SPECTRUM™ 3

A Communicative Course in English

Diane Warshawsky
with Donald R. H. Byrd

Donald R. H. Byrd *Project Director*

Anna Veltfort *Art Director*

Mary Vaughn *Developmental Editor*

Deborah Goldblatt *Project Editor*

 Regents Publishing Company, Inc.

Cover design: Garrett Loubé
Cover photo: Lou Jones, 1983. All rights reserved.
Design assistance: Lisa Schneck
Mechanicals: Regents Production Department

SPECTRUM Textbook 3

SPECTRUM TM is a trademark of Regents Publishing Company, Inc.

10 9 8 7 6 5 4 3 2 1

Published by
Regents Publishing Company, Inc.
2 Park Avenue
New York, N.Y. 10016

Printed in the United States of America
ISBN 0-88345-503-X

Authors

Donald R. H. Byrd *Project director*

Diane Warshawsky *Textbook author*

Sandra Costinett *Textbook author*

Joan Dye *Teacher's edition author*

Nancy Frankfort *Teacher's edition author*

David P. Rein *Workbook author*

Sharon Abrams *Workbook author*

Anna Veltfort *Art direction, page design, and character illustrations*

Consultants

Mercedes Alvarez Lovell *Professor of English, Instituto Ramiro de Maeztu, Madrid, Spain*

Pedro I. Cohen *Professor of English, Linguistics, and Education, University of Panama*

Ikuo Koike *Professor of English and Linguistics, Keio University, Tokyo, Japan*

Nitza Lladó-Torres *Assistant Professor of TESL Graduate School, University of Puerto Rico*

Ana María Payán Ramos *Director, English Teachers College, Escuela Normal Superior, Toluca, Edo. Mexico, Mexico*

Lucy Portela *General Supervisor, Department of Education, San Juan, Puerto Rico*

Barry P. Taylor *Director, English Program for Foreign Students, University of Pennsylvania*

Editorial Staff

Mary Vaughn *Developmental editor*

Deborah Goldblatt *Project editor*

Kathy Niemczyk *Consulting editor*

Cheryl Pavlik *Contributing editor*

Robert Sietsema *Photo editor*

Acknowledgments

Illustrations

All illustrations by Anna Veltfort except the following: pages 4, 34–35, 50–51, 60, 76, 88, 106–107 by Anne Burgess; page 6 by Patrick McDonnell; pages 12, 48, 58–59, 98–99, 116, 122–123 by Kimble Pendleton Mead; pages 26–27, 126–127 by Jim Kinstrey; pages 38, 40, 77, 83–84, 110, 128–129 by Peter Catalanotto; pages 42–43, 52, 61, 90–91, 93, 102, 104, 112, 117 by Arnie Levin; pages 74–75 by Andy Levine; pages 94, 120 by Donna Eshleman.

Photo Credits

Pages 6, 8 *bottom right*, 72 *middle right and bottom right*, 82 *top and bottom*, 83: Robert Sietsema; page 8 *left:* National Zoological Park/Smithsonian Institution/Jessie Cohen, *bottom:* United States Department of Commerce/Maritime Division, *right:* Mexican National Tourist Council, *top:* Florida News Bureau/Department of Commerce/James Gaines; pages 9, 30, 46, 70 *all except far left photo*, 72 *left*, 73, 113, 118 *left*, 124, 125: © Laimute E. Druskis; pages 10, 11, 18, 19, 62 *top*, 63, 66, 67, 70 *far left:* J. Gerard Smith; pages 14, 16: from the collection of Mary Vaughn; pages 20, 29, 61, 64–65, 68, 82 *upper right*, 106: Richard Rodamar; pages 24 *top and middle*, 25, 101 *far left and center left:* Phototeque; page 24 *bottom:* © Lucasfilm Ltd. (LFL) 1977. All rights reserved. Courtesy of Lucasfilm Ltd.; page 26: Library of Congress; page 27: from the collection of L. Milton Warshawsky; page 32: from the collection of Lenore Valeton; page 35 *top:* Canadian Consulate General, *bottom:* Ontario Ministry of Tourism and Recreation; page 40: Japan National Tourist Organization; page 41: Time Magazine/Greg Davis; pages 50–51: © Lou Jones 1982. All rights reserved.; page 54 *top:* © Erika Stone 1983; page 118 *right:* © Erika Stone 1981; pages 54 *bottom*, 64: Harold Goldblatt; page 62 *inset:* The Boston Globe/Steve Haines; page 72 *top right:* Ranjit Ahuja; page 80 *upper left:* Courtesy Pan Am World Airways Inc., *upper right:* French Government Tourist Office, *lower right:* Hawaii Visitors Bureau Photo, *lower left:* Egypt State Tourist Administration/Sobhi Afifi; page 81 *top:* Egypt State Tourist Administration, *bottom:* The Metropolitan Museum of Art/Egyptian Expedition; page 88 *top and bottom:* United States Department of Housing and Urban Development, *middle:* Vermont Travel Division/New England Vacation Center; page 89 *top:* Los Angeles County Museum of Natural History/Western History Collection/A.C. Vroman, *bottom:* United Nations; page 96 *top and middle:* United Press International, *bottom:* National Center for Atmospheric Research/National Science Foundation; page 97 *top:* National Aeronautics and Space Administration, *bottom:* National Oceanic and Atmospheric Administration; page 101 *center right:* National Portrait Gallery/Smithsonian Institution/Washington, D.C./David Iwerks, *far right:* National Portrait Gallery/Smithsonian Institution/Washington, D.C./Gift of Edith A. Scott/Studio of Peter A. and Paul Juley; page 102: Hong Kong Tourist Association/Ray Cranbourne; pages 114–115: MAS; page 126 *top and middle:* Courtesy of Linblad Travel, *bottom:* Courtesy of Linblad Travel/George Holton.

Realia

All realia by Nilda Scherer except the following by Anna Veltfort: page 12; page 17 *top right and bottom right;* page 20 *bottom;* page 29; page 37; page 48; page 66; pages 68–69; page 78; page 82 *top right;* page 86; page 124 *bottom right.*
Page 57: Adapted with permission of SAS.
Page 105: Reprinted with permission of the Campbell Soup Company.

Source Notes

Page 25: *People* magazine, July 20, 1981; page 26: *Statistical Abstract of the United States: 1982–83* (103d ed.), U.S. Bureau of the Census, Washington, D.C., 1982; page 33: *National Geographic*, September 1979; page 34: *Key to Toronto*, March 1983 / *Toronto Life*, March 1983; page 41: *Time*, April 18, 1983; page 49: Hartford, Huntington, *You Are What You Write*, Macmillan, New York, 1973; page 56: Wallechinsky, David, and Wallace, Irving, *The People's Almanac #2*, William Morrow, New York, 1978; page 74: *Mobil Travel Guide (Southwest and South Central Area)*, Rand McNally, Chicago, 1981; page 78: Mesa Verde Museum Association, Inc.; page 81: Wallechinsky, David, and Wallace, Irving, *The People's Almanac #2*, William Morrow, New York, 1978 / Edwards, I.E.S., *The Treasures of Tutankhamun*, Ballantine, New York, 1976 / Desroches-Noblecourt, Christiane, *Tutankhamen: Life and Death of a Pharaoh*, Connoisseur and Michael Joseph Ltd, London, 1963; page 97: Thompson, Philip D., O'Brien, Robert, and the Editors of Time-Life Books, *Weather*, Time-Life Books, New York, 1975; page 113: Miller, Benjamin F., M.D., "The Common Cold," *Family Health Guide and Medical Encyclopedia*, The Reader's Digest Association, Pleasantville, N.Y., 1976.

Contents: *scope and sequence*

Introduction

SPECTRUM is a complete, six-level course in English as a second/foreign language. It is aimed at adults and young adults in secondary schools, universities, and centers for adult education, both in the United States and abroad. SPECTRUM 1 and SPECTRUM 2 are for beginning students. SPECTRUM 1 can be used in classes of zero-level beginners. SPECTRUM 2 reviews and expands all the basic material in SPECTRUM 1 and thus is useful for teaching "false beginners." SPECTRUM 3 and 4 are for intermediate students. SPECTRUM 5 and 6 are for advanced students. Each of the six levels has a fully illustrated textbook with an accompanying teacher's edition, a 96-page workbook, and a four-hour audio program recorded on cassettes.

SPECTRUM has three basic aims: (1) to provide motivating materials that teach students to function in real-life situations in which English is spoken, (2) to teach only authentic English, and (3) to give students a feeling of success and achievement in language learning.

THE COMMUNICATIVE APPROACH TO LANGUAGE TEACHING

SPECTRUM is based on the communicative approach to language teaching. The series teaches basic linguistic *functions* such as *asking for information, talking about feelings, making suggestions*, and *apologizing*. Students practice language that can be put to immediate use. They learn both spoken and written English and the appropriate language for different situations, such as formal speech used with strangers and informal speech with friends. Exercises practice the basic functions and structures. They encourage students to give personal information and express their own ideas and feelings. Natural conversation is stimulated in the classroom.

SPECTRUM recognizes that students can understand more English than they are able to use. This basic distinction between *receptive* and *productive* language allows new language to be systematically introduced before it is practiced. Students need only understand receptive language, which is tested in *right/wrong, multiple choice*, and *matching* exercises. Much of the receptive language becomes productive in later units or levels. Students then actively practice the familiar functions and structures through more challenging *role-playing* and *completion* exercises.

Grammar is carefully graded throughout the series. However, more difficult structures may be introduced *formulaically* when they are needed to perform a given function appropriately. In level 1, students learn expressions such as *Could you spell your last name?* and *May I take a message?*, although the modals *could* and *may* are not analyzed systematically until the intermediate level. In the advanced level, the same structures are expanded further. This system of *preview-review* works as follows:

- Preview: structures are introduced formulaically.
- Analysis: structures are examined and practiced systematically.
- Review: structures are recycled for further practice.

Useful *formulas*, such as *How do you do* and *Nice meeting you*, are also taught in SPECTRUM, without analyzing their structure.

THE TEXTBOOK

There are sixteen units in the textbook, two of which are review. Each of the other fourteen units contains eight pages and is divided into five major sections: (1) *Try this* (warm-up) and conversations—first and second pages; (2) *Ways to say it* (functions and grammar)—third, fourth, and fifth pages; (3) Comprehension dialogue and *Listen in* (listening)—sixth page; (4) *Your turn* (free conversation activity) and *Say it right* (pronunciation)—seventh page; and (5) *On your own* (reading)—eighth page.

The *Try this* section is an oral activity in which students use grammar, functions, and vocabulary they have studied in previous levels or units. Students may role-play a situation or discuss information given in a short article. The activity is intended not only to review familiar language but also to motivate students to learn more sophisticated ways of performing a function or discussing a topic. The conversations that follow present new language students can use to do this. The conversations are first presented receptively. Students then test their understanding of the new functions and grammar through receptive *Figure it out* exercises.

Students then move from reception to production on the *Ways to say it* pages. Here they practice short functional dialogues based on the language in the conversations and, when appropriate, longer dialogues that combine related functions. Vocabulary is expanded and alternative answers to questions are given, allowing students to exchange personal information and give opinions. *Close-up* or grammar exercises follow selected dialogues and enable students to practice the structures introduced in the unit as they appear. Exercises are contextualized and natural language is used.

The comprehension dialogue is a receptive activity that introduces more complex language and develops a story line. Students listen to and read the dialogue, which is followed by a receptive *Figure it out* exercise. The dialogues provide more challenging material, and students need not produce the language in them. This page also contains a receptive listening activity *(Listen in)*.

The *Your turn* page gives students a chance to engage in meaningful free conversation. A variety of photos or artwork suggest different topics for discussion. Here students can draw on their personal experiences and perform a wide number of functions. Students not only practice the new language in the unit but are free to use any of the language learned so far. This page also contains a pronunciation activity *(Say it right)*.

On your own is a reading activity where students read for both information and pleasure. Authentic newspaper and magazine articles, letters, and other human-interest selections are included.

THE TEACHER'S EDITION

The teacher's edition of the textbook gives step-by-step instructions for all exercises; suggestions for additional activities; answer keys; the script for all *Listen in* activities; and cultural, usage, and pronunciation notes. An answer key for workbook exercises and the scripts for workbook listening activities are also included.

A *Purpose* page begins every unit of the teacher's edition. It states the objectives of the unit and lists the functions and forms that are taught. It also presents suggestions for lesson plans.

THE WORKBOOK

Each unit of the workbook reinforces the functions, structures, and vocabulary taught in the corresponding textbook unit. Familiar material is presented in new contexts. The workbook focuses on developing listening and writing skills. Each unit also contains a reading selection and an activity devoted to conversation.

THE AUDIO PROGRAM

The audio program records the conversations which begin each textbook unit, the comprehension dialogues, the *Listen in*, and the *Say it right* activities. In addition, all listening activities in the workbook are recorded. All dialogues on the audio program have been recorded at normal conversational speed, and feature authentic-sounding voices and sound effects. A cassette symbol appears next to each section of the textbook and workbook which is recorded.

1. Taking off

These people have just run into each other at the airport in Columbus, Ohio. Read the information about them and then act out the conversation following the steps below.

Kim Richards is going back to the University of Texas, where she's an engineering student. Peter Smith, a friend of hers from school, comes up and talks to her. He's also majoring in engineering. He's with his brother Steve, who owns a bookstore in Columbus.

1. Peter and Kim greet each other.
2. Peter introduces his brother Steve to Kim.
3. Kim and Steve talk about what they do.
4. Kim introduces Peter and Steve to her mother.
5. Peter offers to help Kim with her luggage.

United Airlines Flight 461 is flying from Columbus to Chicago.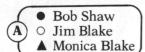

(A) ● Bob Shaw
○ Jim Blake
▲ Monica Blake

● Hi, Jim! Where are you off to?
○ Oh, Bob, hi! We're taking a few days off and going to Chicago. Say, I hear you bought a house.
● Yes, as a matter of fact, we just moved in over the weekend.
○ Well, business must be pretty good. *(To Monica)* Bob has his own computer business.
▲ Oh, really?
○ By the way, have you two met each other?
▲ No, I don't believe we have.
○ Monica, this is Bob Shaw. Bob, my wife, Monica.
● How do you do, Monica.
▲ Glad to meet you, Bob.
(Over loudspeaker: United Airlines Flight 461 to Chicago is now boarding at Gate 9. Flight 461 . . .)
○ Oh, there's our flight.
● I've got a plane to catch, too. Enjoy yourselves in Chicago!
○ Thanks, we will.

B ● Doug Lee
○ Laura Enders

● I see you're reading *Eye of the Needle*. How do you like it?
○ I can't put it down. Have you read it?
● Yes. As a matter of fact, I just finished it. The ending's great. . . .
○ Don't tell me! I only have fifty pages to go.
● Are you from Chicago?
○ Well, I'm originally from Columbus, but I live in Chicago now.
● How do you like it?
○ Very much. Have you ever been there before?
● No, I haven't. This is my first trip. I have a job interview. By the way, my name's Doug Lee.
○ I'm Laura Enders.

C

● Here, let me help you get that down.
○ Oh, thanks. That's really nice of you.
● Well, it's been nice talking to you.
○ I've enjoyed talking to you, too. Good luck on your interview.
● Thanks. I'll need it.

Figure it out

1. Say *Right*, *Wrong*, or *I don't know*.

1. Bob and Jim know each other.   *Right*.
2. Bob and Monica met before this conversation.
3. Jim and Monica have been to Chicago before.
4. Doug Lee was in Chicago a year ago.
5. Doug is reading *Eye of the Needle*.
6. Laura doesn't like *Eye of the Needle*.

2. Do the sentences in each pair mean the same thing or is their meaning different? Say *Same* or *Different*.

1. Where are you off to?   *Same*.
   Where are you going?

2. I just finished it.
   I finished it a long time ago.

3. Bob has his own company.
   Bob owns a company.

4. We're taking Monday off.
   We're going to work Monday.

5. Have you been to Chicago before?
   Is this your first trip to Chicago?

6. Have fun!
   Enjoy yourselves!

Ways to say it

Act out the short conversations on the next three pages. First practice a conversation as it is given. Then practice it again, substituting personal information or the information provided for the words in *italics*. When there are two choices for a response (*Yes, we have* or *No, we haven't*), give the one that applies to you. When there is more than one way to say something, the alternatives are given like this:

| No, I haven't. |
| No, I don't believe I have. |

The *Close-up* sections present the new structures in grammar "frames." After studying a frame, do the exercise that follows.

---

1 INTRODUCE SOMEONE

The people on the right are all waiting at the airport to take United Flight 461. Read the information about each one.

Which people know each other? Fill in the blanks below.

_____ and _____ both teach at Taft High School.
_____ and _____ are from the same hometown.
_____ and _____ used to work together.
_____ and _____ went to college together.

You are also a passenger, and you know all five people. Introduce the people who don't know each other. Other students will play the roles of the five people.

● Hi, *Sara.*

● Have you met *John?*
○ Yes, I have. We *both teach at Taft High School.*

> John Roy teaches French at Taft High. He's from Troy, Ohio.

> Elaine Simon has her own travel agency. She grew up with John in Troy, Ohio.

> Sara Rivera teaches Spanish at Taft High. She worked with Elaine ten years ago.

> Martha Jones has her own advertising agency. She went to Ohio State from 1960 to 1964.

> Ted Grant has his own computer business. He knew Martha at Ohio State.

● Have you met *Martha?*
○ No, | I haven't. |
       | I don't believe I have. |

● *Sara,* I'd like you to meet *Martha Jones. Martha has her own advertising agency. Martha, Sara Rivera....*

---

2 **Find out if two students in the class know each other. If they don't, introduce them.**

● Have you two met (each other)?
○ Yes, (we have). *We were in the same English class last term.*
○ No, we haven't.
● *Carla,* this is *Roger Duval....*

This is . . . is less formal than I'd like you to meet . . .

---

3 TALK ABOUT PLACES YOU'VE BEEN

Been means "gone" in this context and thus is followed by *to.*

● Have you (ever) been to *Chicago?*
○ Yes, *(I've been there) many times.*
○ No, I never have.
○ Have you?
● Yes, *I was just there last week.*
● No, I haven't (either).

I've been there	once.
	twice.
	a few times.
	many times.

| I was just there last week. |
| I just got back from there. |

4

PRESENT PERFECT

Yes-no questions and short answers

Have	I you we they	met	Roger?
Has	he she		

Yes,	I you we they	have.
No,		haven't.
Yes,	he	has.
No,	she	hasn't.

Some past participles of irregular verbs

Base form	Past form	Past participle
be (am, is, are)	was, were	been
do	did	done
eat	ate	eaten
go	went	gone
have	had	had
leave	left	left
meet	met	met
read [riyd]	read [red]	read [red]
see	saw	seen

See p. 134 for a list of more irregular verbs.

5 **Complete each conversation with a question and a short answer in the present perfect. Use the verbs in parentheses.**

1. ● I see you're reading *Shōgun.*
   ○ Yes. _*Have you read it?*_ (read)
   ● _____, but I'd like to.

2. ● What are you eating?
   ○ Guacamole. It's Mexican.
   _____ before? (have)
   ● _____. Is it good?
   ○ Delicious. Here, try some.

3. ● Where's Ellen? _____ already? (leave)
   ○ _____. She went home an hour ago.

4. ● John's going to France.
   ○ Oh, really? _____ before? (be)
   ● _____. This is his second or third trip.

5. ● I can't find my keys. _____? (see)
   ○ _____. Sorry.

6. ● We're going to lunch now. What about you and Bob? _____? (eat)
   ○ _____.
   ● Then why don't you join us?
   ○ We'd love to.

6 TALK ABOUT THE RECENT PAST

● I hear you *found an apartment.*
○ Yes, as a matter of fact, I *just moved in over the weekend.*

Just, like frequency adverbs, follows forms of the verb *be* (and other auxiliaries) but precedes the simple past (and the simple present):

I was *just* there.
I *just* got back from there.

I hear you . . .	Yes, I . . .
found an apartment.	finished my exams two days ago.
know Carol James.	moved in over the weekend.
go to Detroit a lot.	was at her house last night.
got a new job.	started this morning.
go to Ohio State.	was there last week.

5

- Here, let me help you *get that down*.
○ Thanks a lot. That's really nice of you.

Let me help you . . .

1. get that down.   a
2. put that up.   b
3. carry those.   c
4. move that.   d

Ways you've said it

Would you like some help with . . . ?

Act out the conversation. Play Role A or Role B. Then end it with one or more expressions from the box below.

Some ways to end a conversation

Enjoy yourself (yourselves)!
Enjoy your trip (your stay)!
It's been nice talking to you.
I've enjoyed talking to you.

Ways you've said it

Have fun! (informal)
Have a good time! (informal)

Role A

You go into a café in Austin, Texas, and sit down at a table next to someone who's reading the Italian newspaper, *La Stampa*. Strike up a conversation and tell him or her about yourself. Find out:

1. where the person is from.
2. if this is his or her first trip to the United States.
3. what kind of work he or she does.

Start like this: *I see you're reading La Stampa. . . .*

Role B

You're sitting in a café in Austin, Texas, and the person at the table next to you starts a conversation. Here is some information you can use:

1. You live in Milan, Italy, but you were born in Turin.
2. This is your third trip to the United States, but it's your first trip to Austin. You're here on business.
3. You own a small publishing company in Milan.

Find out if the person next to you has ever been to Italy.

How have you been?

Laura Enders runs into an old friend in a parking lot.

1

Roger: Laura!
Laura: Oh, hi, Roger. How have you been?
Roger: Fine. I hear you went back to Columbus for a few days.
Laura: Yes. I just got back yesterday.
Roger: Did you have a nice visit?
Laura: Really nice. It was good being home and just relaxing. My brother Mark was there, too. You've met Mark, haven't you?
Roger: Sure. I met him when he was here in Chicago last year. What's he up to these days? Still playing the guitar?
Laura: Yes, as a matter of fact, he just started his own band with some of his friends. How's everything with you and Peg?
Roger: Great.
Laura: How are the kids?
Roger: They're both fine.
Laura: I haven't seen them in so long. They must be really big.
Roger: Well, why don't you come over sometime? Peg and the kids would love to see you.
Laura: I'll do that. I'll give Peg a call during the week.

2. Figure it out

Say *Right*, *Wrong*, or *I don't know*.

1. Laura was in Columbus for four days.
   I don't know.
2. Laura's brother Mark has been to Chicago.
3. Mark plays the guitar in a friend's band.
4. Mark just started to play the guitar.
5. Roger and Peg have two children.
6. Laura just saw Roger and Peg's children.

3. Listen in

Read the statement below. Then listen to another conversation taking place in the parking lot and choose *a*, *b*, or *c*.

These people are talking about _____.
a. a book
b. a movie
c. a restaurant

7

Your turn

These photographs show places you possibly have visited and things you possibly have seen or done in your life. Discuss your experiences in groups. Ask your classmates about their experiences, and then tell them about yours.

- *Have you ever been to Mexico City?*
- ○ *Yes, I have.*
- *Really? When did you go?*
- ○ *Last summer. I went with some friends.*
- *How did you like it?*
- ○ *It was very beautiful. What about you? Have you ever been there?*
- *No, I haven't, but I'd like to go there someday.*

Many people love to ride the roller coaster in amusement parks.

Mexico City is the third largest city in the world.

There are very few pandas living outside of their native China. Here is the famous panda Ling-Ling, now at the National Zoo in Washington, D.C.

Agatha Christie is one of the most popular authors of mystery novels.

People today generally travel long distances by plane, but some people still travel by ocean liner. The S.S. United States was once the fastest ocean liner in the world.

Say it right

Say the past participles below. Then ask questions using the phrases on the right. 📼

been	[bin]	. . . been to South America?
seen	[siyn]	. . . seen a Japanese film?
gone	[gɔn]	. . . gone to a soccer game?

had	[hæd]	. . . had Chinese food?
eaten	[íytṇ]	. . . eaten frogs' legs?
read	[red]	. . . read a Hemingway novel?

- *Have you ever been to South America?*
- ○ *Yes, I have. (No, I haven't.)*

On your own

Peter Novak
High school teacher
Grand Forks, North Dakota

I've never gone swimming in the ocean before, so I have no idea what it's like to be in salt water or to swim in high waves. As a matter of fact, I've never even *seen* the ocean, except in pictures. I've lived in North Dakota all my life, and both the Atlantic and the Pacific are over a thousand miles away. I've always swum in freshwater lakes. I've gone swimming in Lake Superior once or twice, but I think it must be more exciting to swim in the ocean.

Luigi Contini
Computer programmer
Rome, Italy

I've always wanted to act in a play. I've never been on stage before, not even when I was in school, but my job has nothing to do with acting. There's a theater group in my neighborhood, and I've often thought of joining it. I have this secret desire to get up in front of thousands of people and then get wild applause. I guess everyone dreams about being a star.

Cornelia Valentine
Commercial artist
Oakland, California

I think it would be great to go up in a hot-air balloon. I've seen pictures of people traveling in balloons and it looks like a lot of fun. The view must be fantastic from up there. I've even heard of people crossing the ocean in balloons. It sounds amazing, doesn't it? Of course, I've been on planes, but that's not the same. I suppose that going up in a balloon is dangerous, but I'd like to try it anyway.

Patricia Vera
Bookkeeper
Santiago, Chile

That's a difficult question because there are a lot of things I've never done. . . . I guess I'd like to do physical work for a living, maybe construction work. I've worked for a construction company for the last ten years, but I'm a bookkeeper and I sit at a desk all day. Sometimes I'd like to be outside actually working on the buildings. I bet I'd feel more relaxed at night. Maybe I could even lose some weight. I've gained a pound every year since I started this job.

Say *Right* or *Wrong*.

1. Peter Novak has never gone swimming in salt water.   *Right.*
2. Lake Superior is a freshwater lake.
3. Everyone working for a construction company does hard physical work.
4. Patricia Vera has gained ten pounds working for a construction company.
5. Luigi Contini has a secret desire to be a star.
6. When people really like a play, there is wild applause.
7. Cornelia Valentine has never been in a hot-air balloon because it's too dangerous.
8. It is possible to travel long distances in a balloon.

Words

See p. 5 for a list of past participles of irregular verbs.

It's been nice talking to you.	advertising agency	ocean liner	I hear . . .	each other
I've enjoyed talking to you.	frog	amusement park	Let me help you . . .	both
I don't believe I have.	hometown	mystery novel	major in	same
as a matter of fact	publishing company	Have you ever. . . ?	get something down	just
Enjoy yourself (yourselves)!	just	on business	put something up	beautiful
engineering	panda	I see . . .	his/her own	someday

Students Look for Jobs

CLINTON, April 15— It seems as if everyone is looking for a job, and Clinton High School students are no exception. Anne Rutgers, a teacher at the school, reports that most of her students are trying to find work this summer. "They're not doing it just for fun or to have something to do, but because they have to," said Rutgers, adding that some of them have been saving money for college for a year or two.

Donna Lucas, in her third year at Clinton, has found a job as a file clerk. "I've done office work for the last two summers," she said. "It's a little boring at times, but it's a change from school-work."

Jim Wright, also a junior, says he wanted to do construction work like his older brother, but he couldn't find a job. Instead he's going to be a waiter at a local restaurant. "I'm not sure if I'll like it or not," said Jim, who has never worked as a waiter before. "I'll let you know at the end of the summer."

Some students want to work for the experience rather than for the money. Claire Metzger is one such student.

1. Read the article. Then choose a partner and discuss the questions:

1. What do high school students in your country usually do during vacation?
2. Do high school students ever have jobs then? If so, what kinds of jobs do they have? Do they work part-time or full-time?

2. Find out if your partner has ever had a job during vacation. If so, discuss these questions:

1. What kind(s) of job(s) did your partner have?
2. Did your partner enjoy the job(s)?

3. Find out what your partner does now. If your partner is working, find out when he or she started the job.

Tina Marco is starting a summer job as a waitress at Frank's Restaurant.

Ⓐ ● Marge
⚬ Tina

● Hi. You must be the new waitress. I'm Marge.
⚬ Hi, Marge. I'm Tina.
● Do you go to Clinton High, Tina?
⚬ I'll start this fall. I've only lived here since the beginning of June.
● Really? Where did you live before?
⚬ Gary.
● Well, welcome to Clinton, then.
⚬ Thanks.

Ⓑ

⚬ How long have you lived in Clinton?
● Me? My whole life! You know Frank, the owner? We've known each other for thirty-five years . . . since kindergarten.
⚬ No kidding! Have you ever wanted to live somewhere else?
● When I was younger, I wanted to move to Hollywood and be an actress. But here I am . . . still in Clinton and still a waitress.
⚬ Oh, that's funny. I've always wanted to be an actress, too. How long have you been a waitress?
● For twenty years now.
⚬ That's a long time!
● You're telling me! I've always wanted to try a different kind of work. I make good money as a waitress, though, so I just never have.
⚬ Where else have you worked, or have you always worked here?
● Oh, no. Frank's only had this place since 1978. Before that, I worked at the Clinton Hotel.

been a waitress?

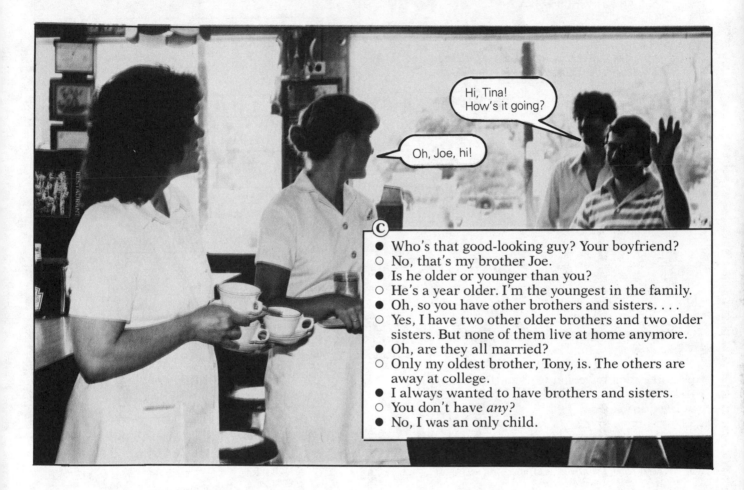

Hi, Tina! How's it going?

Oh, Joe, hi!

C

● Who's that good-looking guy? Your boyfriend?
○ No, that's my brother Joe.
● Is he older or younger than you?
○ He's a year older. I'm the youngest in the family.
● Oh, so you have other brothers and sisters. . . .
○ Yes, I have two other older brothers and two older sisters. But none of them live at home anymore.
● Oh, are they all married?
○ Only my oldest brother, Tony, is. The others are away at college.
● I always wanted to have brothers and sisters.
○ You don't have *any?*
● No, I was an only child.

Figure it out

1. Say *Right, Wrong,* or *I don't know.*

1. Tina moved to Clinton in June. *Right.*
2. Tina has never been a waitress before.
3. Marge and Frank met each other thirty-five years ago.
4. Frank opened the restaurant in 1978.
5. Joe is Tina's oldest brother.
6. When Marge was younger, she lived in Hollywood.
7. Both of Tina's sisters are in college.

2. Fill in the blanks with *for* or *since.*

I've lived here . . .

1. ___*for*___ 35 years.
2. _____ 1978.
3. _____ June.
4. _____ a month.

3. Match.

1. Tina lived in Gary when she was a child.
2. Tina has lived in Clinton for a month.
3. Marge worked at the Clinton Hotel from 1965 to 1978.
4. Marge has worked at Frank's since 1978.

a. She still does.
b. She doesn't anymore.

Ways to say it

1 TALK ABOUT WHERE YOU'VE LIVED

● How long have you lived in *Clinton*?

○ For *three years*.
  Since *1982*.

○ My whole life.
  All my life.

● Where did you live before?
○ *Gary*.

For . . .	Since . . .
three years.	1982.
about a year and a half.	the beginning of the year.
a few months.	the end of June.
a long time.	August.
	last spring.

▲

For is used before a *period* of time.
Since is used before a *point* in time.

The seasons in the Northern Hemisphere	
Spring	March 21 or 22 to June 20
Summer	June 21 or 22 to September 22
Fall (Autumn)	September 23 to December 21
Winter	December 22 to March 20

2 TALK ABOUT JOBS PRESENT AND PAST

● What do you do?
○ I'm a *waitress* at *Frank's Restaurant*.
● Oh, how long have you worked there?
○ (For) *seven* years. (Before that I worked at *the Clinton Hotel*.)

```
Frank Sylvester    821-4325
525 W. Deming Place    Chicago, Illinois  60614

Position desired:  Hairdresser

Experience:        The New Wave  Hairdresser, 1982-present
                   Cut 'n' Curl  Hairdresser, 1978-1982
                   The Hair Inn  Hairdresser, 1974-1978
```

```
Jean Jacobs    588-7221
2519 Ross Road    Silver Spring, Maryland  20910

Professional
experience:  1976-present  Sales manager, Cullison Plastics
             1964-1976     Salesclerk, Cullison Plastics

Education:   M.B.A.  University of Maryland, 1975
```

```
Marge Hillcrest    782-6308
1121 North End Avenue    Clinton, Indiana  46404

Experience:  1978-present  Waitress, Frank's Restaurant
             1965-1978     Waitress, Clinton Hotel

Education:   Clinton Junior College, 1964-65
```

3 TALK ABOUT HOW LONG YOU'VE KNOWN SOMEONE

● How long have you and *Frank* known each other?

○ For *thirty-five years*.   ○ We just met *last week*.

▲

Base form:	know
Past form:	knew
Past participle:	known

4 TALK ABOUT YOUR FANTASIES

● I've always wanted to *go to Italy and study opera*.
○ *When I was younger, I wanted to move to Hollywood and be an actress*.

I've always wanted to be a rock star.

5 Close-up

PRESENT PERFECT

Information questions

How long	have	you they	worked [t]	at Frank's?	
			lived [d]	here?	
	has	he she	wanted [əd]	to move?	

▲ The past participle of regular verbs is the same as the past tense form.

Affirmative statements

I We They	've	worked	at Frank's	for three years. since 1982.
		lived	here	
He She	's	wanted	to move	

▲
have ▶ 've
has ▶ 's
he's = he is or he has
she's = she is or she has

Present perfect vs. past tense

Use the present perfect to refer to something that began in the past and continues into the present. *For* or *since* show the duration of the event. Use the past tense to refer to something that was completed in the past. Compare:

I've worked at Frank's since 1978. (I work at Frank's now.)
I worked at Frank's from 1975 to 1978. (I don't work at Frank's anymore.)
I've studied English for three years. (I'm still studying English.)
I studied English when I was younger. (I'm not studying English anymore.)

6 Combine each pair of sentences into a single sentence, using the present perfect and *for* or *since*.

1. I know Lois Ray.
   I met her ten years ago.
   I've known Lois Ray for ten years.

2. I'm at the Clinton Hotel now.
   I got here at 2:00.

3. Debra works at the Kingsley School.
   She got the job in September.

4. Doris has her own travel agency.
   She started it a long time ago.

5. We want to live in Seattle.
   We first wanted to move there in 1965.

6. The Smiths live in Denver now.
   They moved there last spring.

7 Now ask a question beginning with *How long ... ?* about each item in exercise 6. Another student will answer your questions.

● *How long have you known Lois Ray?*
○ *I've known her for ten years. . . .*

8 TALK ABOUT YOUR FAMILY

● Do you have any brothers and sisters?

○ I have *three older brothers and two older sisters.* (I'm the *youngest* in the family.)

○ No, I was an only child.

I'm the *youngest* in the family. =
My brothers and sisters are older than I am.
I'm the *oldest* in the family. =
My brothers and sisters are younger than I am.

---

9  PARTITIVES, *THE OTHER ONE*, AND *THE OTHERS*

Jim Martin has four brothers.	All of them are married. None of them live in Clinton. Two of them live in Chicago. The others live in California.
He has two sisters.	Both of them are in college. One of them lives at home. The other one lives at school.
He has lots of cousins.	Most of them live in California. Many of them were born there. Some of them moved there from Clinton.

The expression *none of them* may be followed by either a singular or a plural verb.

---

10 Jim Martin has a big family. Read about his family in *Close-up* frame 9. Then answer these questions using the information in the frame, and a partitive expression, *the other one*, or *the others*.

1. Are Jim's brothers married or single?
   All of them are married.
2. Where do Jim's sisters live?
3. What do Jim's sisters do?
4. Where do Jim's brothers live?
5. Where do Jim's cousins live?
6. Did any of Jim's cousins ever live in Clinton?

I see from your résumé . . .

Bill Dow is interviewing Doug Lee for a job as the director of a recreation program for teenagers. Mr. Dow runs the Community Services Agency. 🔲

1

Mr. Dow: Well, Mr. Lee, I see from your résumé that you've had quite a lot of experience in the shoe business.

Doug: Yes, my father has a shoe store, and I used to work there after school.

Mr. Dow: What kind of work have you done with adolescents?

Doug: Well, I taught swimming for a couple of summers at a camp. A lot of the campers were in their early teens. Then I taught high school physical education, and I've been a guidance counselor in the Columbus public school system for the last three years.

Mr. Dow: Why are you thinking of leaving your present job?

Doug: Well, I enjoy counseling, but I miss athletics. This job would give me a chance to do both of them. And I feel, too, that I'm ready for a change. I've lived in Columbus my whole life.

Mr. Dow: So you think you'd like living in Chicago?

Doug: Very much. I've always wanted to live in a big city.

Mr. Dow: Well, Mr. Lee, you seem to have some good qualifications for the job. We're interviewing this whole week, so I'll let you know one way or the other in ten days or so. While you're here, I'd also like you to meet . . . (*Knock at the door*)

2. Figure it out

Say *Right*, *Wrong*, or *I don't know*.

1. Doug used to teach swimming.   *Right*.
2. Doug is a guidance counselor now.
3. Doug likes sports.
4. Doug doesn't like big cities.
5. Doug has worked with teenagers before.
6. Mr. Dow will call or write Doug in about ten days.
7. Mr. Dow is going to interview two other people for the job.

3. Listen in 🔲

Kate Simmons is a social worker at the Community Services Agency. Read the questions below. Then listen to the conversation and answer them.

1. How long has Kate worked at the Community Services Agency?
2. How long have Kate and Doug known each other?
3. Where did they meet?

Your turn

Phyllis Sandler

Awards and Activities: President—Great Books Club,
Sarah Davis Science Award
Best Quality: Good conversationalist
Likes: People, people, people
Dislikes: Staying up late at night
Ambition: To visit a new country every year
People say: *"She's got a great sense of humor, even about herself." "She's extremely patient—she explained chemistry to me."*

David Simon

Awards and Activities: Marathon Champion,
Secretary—Great Books Club
Best Quality: Fantastic memory
Likes: Learning about new things
Dislikes: Making conversation with people he doesn't know
Ambition: To save money to buy a small country house
People say: *"He's incredibly well organized. I always borrowed his notes." "He seems shy, but he's fun."*

Melina Spanos

Awards and Activities: Best Actress, President—French Club
Best Quality: Common sense
Likes: New people, new places
Dislikes: Doing the same thing every day
Ambition: To retire early and write a book
People say: *"She's a great listener. People always tell her their problems . . . and she never repeats anything." "She feels comfortable in the most difficult situations."*

Victor Suarez

Awards and Activities: Captain—Football Team
Best Quality: Honesty
Likes: Anything exciting
Dislikes: Being alone
Ambition: To make some money and retire when he's
still young
People say: *"He's not afraid of anything." "He's always helping other people."*

Here's a page from the 1965 Clinton High School Yearbook. All of the people went to college after graduating from high school, and they are all now very successful in their professions. One is a firefighter, one is a librarian, one is a teacher, and one is an international spy. Read about the people, and then work in groups to guess their professions. Discuss the reasons for your choices.

Say it right

Say the words below. Then practice the conversation.

talked   studied   started
  [t]   [d]   [əd]

● Have you talked to Mary?
○ Yes, I talked to her last night.
● Has she started her music class?

○ Yes, she started it last week.
● Has she studied music before?
○ Yes, she studied it when she was younger.

On your own

**Read the advertisement, the résumé, and the letter.
Then say *Right*, *Wrong*, or *I don't know*.**

1. Carmen has worked at a publishing company.
   Right.
2. Carmen has always lived in New York.
3. Carmen has always wanted to work at an
   advertising agency.
4. Carmen has some design experience.
5. Carmen only knows a little Spanish.
6. The art department at LPS designs a lot of
   Spanish ads.

ADVERTISING/DESIGN

Major advertising agency needs a graphic designer to
work in growing art department. Good salary and benefits. Opportunity for advancement. Some previous
design experience required. Knowledge of Spanish
helpful. Send résumé to:

David Carlson
Personnel Manager
LPS Advertising
P.O. Box 1082
New York, NY 10003

RÉSUMÉ

Carmen Ortiz   (212) 998-7094
1350 Ocean Parkway   Brooklyn, NY 11230

EXPERIENCE   Design assistant, Whitman Publishing Co.
             1983-present

EDUCATION   B.A. Commercial Art
             University of Maryland, 1983

             H.S. Diploma, Northwood High School
             Silver Spring, Maryland, 1979

SPECIAL   Fluent in Spanish
SKILLS

OTHER   Part-time bilingual secretary
EMPLOYMENT   Long Life Insurance Co.
             Washington, D.C., 1981-82

             Waitress, Parkside Restaurant
             Silver Spring, Maryland, 1977-79

                              1350 Ocean Parkway
                              Brooklyn, NY 11230
                              June 21, 1985
Mr. David Carlson
Personnel Manager
LPS Advertising
P.O. Box 1082
New York, NY 10003

Dear Mr. Carlson:

I would like to apply for the graphic design
position that you advertised in The New York Times
on June 20. I have been a design assistant at
Whitman Publishing Company for the past two years.
I am very interested in advertising. I have a B.A.
in Commercial Art, and I have taken courses in
advertising design. I also speak Spanish fluently.

If you would like me to come in for an interview,
please call me at (212) 998-7094. I have enclosed
a copy of my résumé. Thank you for your attention.

Sincerely yours,

Carmen Ortiz

Carmen Ortiz

Words   See p. 12 for a list of seasons and p. 14 for a list of partitive expressions.

How long . . . ?	end	hairdresser	librarian	oldest	the others
my whole life	travel agency	sales manager	spy	youngest	known (knew)
all my life	an only child	salesclerk	for/since	international	
beginning	cousin	firefighter	a long time	the other one	

3. Some of us are

Are you going to be around this weekend?

Yes. I think so.

Try this

Read the ad. Then continue Mark's conversation with Shelley.

Mark

You have two tickets to the Lena Horne concert for Saturday night. Invite Shelley to go with you. If she's been to the concert, ask her opinion of it.

Shelley

You went to the Lena Horne concert last night and really enjoyed it. Mark has two tickets. Decide if you want to go again. If not, suggest a student in the class that Mark can invite.

Some friends are making plans for the weekend.

(A)
- ● Claire
- ○ Janet
- ▲ Charlie

- ● Anything exciting going on this weekend?
- ○ Oh, look, Lena Horne's in town.
- ▲ Who's Lena Horne? I've never heard of her.
- ○ What? She's one of the greatest singers alive today.
- ● The tickets must cost a fortune. Are there any good movies?
- ○ Well, there's *E.T.*
- ● Hey, I've heard that's excellent. Why don't we go Saturday night?
- ▲ I've already seen it.
- ● You have?
- ▲ I just saw it the night before last.
- ● Was it any good?
- ▲ *I* thought so. I think it's Spielberg's best film.

Janet   Claire   Charlie

getting together.

B

○ Let's see what's playing at the State. Oh, look. . . *Tootsie*. It's supposed to be really funny.
● Fine with me. Charlie?
▲ We could go dancing.
○ Listen. I think we'll have to talk later. I've got to go now.

C ● Claire
○ Greg

● Are you free Saturday night?
○ I might not be in town. I'm not sure yet. A friend invited me to visit him in Boston.
● Well, some of us are getting together, and I thought you might want to come, too.
○ What are you thinking of doing?
● We haven't decided yet for sure. We might go dancing, but we'll probably go see *Tootsie*.
○ Oh, I haven't seen it yet.
● Well, come then.
○ Sure, if I'm in town. I'll call you and let you know.

Figure it out

1. Say *Right*, *Wrong*, or *I don't know*.

1. Lena Horne is a famous singer.   *Right*.
2. The tickets to the Lena Horne concert are probably expensive.
3. Charlie liked *E.T.*
4. Janet has seen *Tootsie*.   *Wrong*
5. Greg is going to be out of town Saturday night.
6. Claire and her friends are going to the movies Saturday night.
7. Greg doesn't want to see *Tootsie*.

2. Find another way to say it.

1. two nights ago   *the night before last*
2. What did you think of it?
3. We haven't decided, but we will.
4. I'll tell you.
5. a lot of money
6. I've heard it's really funny.
7. Maybe we'll go dancing.

Ways to say it

This week's movies

Movie Ratings
****	Excellent
***	Good
**	Fair
*	Poor

**** **E.T., The Extra-Terrestrial.** Steven Spielberg has created a classic. The whole family will enjoy this fantasy about a boy who befriends a creature from outer space. (State)

**** **Tootsie.** One of the best and funniest films of the year. Dustin Hoffman is an unemployed actor who plays the role of a woman to get a job. Hoffman gives one of the greatest performances of his career. (Liberty)

*** **Chan is Missing.** This low-budget black-and-white film takes you on a marvelous trip through San Francisco's Chinatown. (Cinema Two)

* **One Horse Town.** The best acting comes from the horse in this tired Western directed by Terence Clay. Save your money. (Fox)

1 | GIVE AN OPINION

● Are there any good movies in town?
○ Well, there's _E.T._ at the _State_.

● Oh, it's supposed to be _excellent_. Why don't we go?

● Oh, not _E.T._ I've heard it's not that _great_. See what's playing at the _Liberty_.

hear
heard
heard

● I've never heard of it. Is it any good?

I've heard it is.
It's supposed to be.

2

● I (just) _read Iris Murdoch's_ | latest / new | _novel._
○ Was it any good?

● I thought so.   ● I didn't think so.

Ways you've said it
What did you think of it?
How did you like it?
How was it?

Michael Jackson
Thriller

Marsha Norman
'night, Mother

an album

a novel

a play

20

3 (TALK ABOUT PLANS)

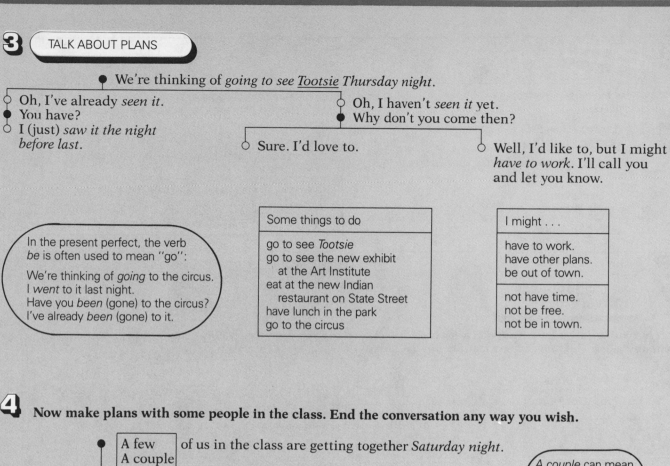

● We're thinking of *going to see* <u>Tootsie</u> *Thursday night*.

○ Oh, I've already *seen it*.
● You have?
○ I (just) *saw it the night before last*.

○ Oh, I haven't *seen it* yet.
● Why don't you come then?

○ Sure. I'd love to.

○ Well, I'd like to, but I might *have to work*. I'll call you and let you know.

In the present perfect, the verb *be* is often used to mean "go":

We're thinking of *going* to the circus.
I *went* to it last night.
Have you *been* (gone) to the circus?
I've already *been* (gone) to it.

Some things to do

go to see *Tootsie*
go to see the new exhibit
   at the Art Institute
eat at the new Indian
   restaurant on State Street
have lunch in the park
go to the circus

I might . . .

have to work.
have other plans.
be out of town.

not have time.
not be free.
not be in town.

4 Now make plans with some people in the class. End the conversation any way you wish.

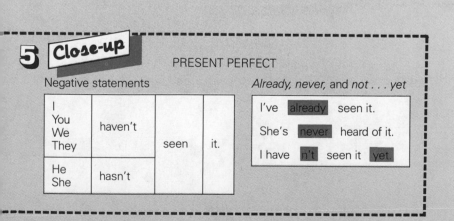

● A few / A couple / Some of us in the class are getting together *Saturday night*.

Do you want to join us?
○ What are you thinking of doing?

● We're going to *see* <u>E.T.</u> . . .

● We haven't decided yet (for sure).
We're not sure yet.

A couple can mean "exactly two" or "two or three."

We might *go dancing*. . . .

5 **Close-up**

PRESENT PERFECT

Negative statements

I You We They	haven't	seen	it.
He She	hasn't		

Already, never, and *not . . . yet*

I've already seen it.

She's never heard of it.

I have n't seen it yet.

6 | **Close-up**   PRESENT PERFECT VS. PAST TENSE

Use the present perfect to refer to an *unspecified* time in the past:
 	
   Have you seen *E.T.*?
   Yes. I've already seen it.
 	
Use the past tense to refer to a *specific* time in the past:
 	
   When did you see it?
   I saw it last week.
	Use present perfect negative statements to refer to something that didn't happen in the past but still might happen. Compare:
	
	   I haven't seen *E.T.* (But I might see it.)
	   I didn't see *E.T.* when it was here. (It's not playing anymore.)
	
	Use *yet* when you expect something to happen:
	
	   Have you seen *E.T.* yet?
	   I haven't seen *E.T.* yet. (But I plan to see it.)

7 (TALK ABOUT THINGS YOU'VE DONE)

You're visiting Tokyo for a week and a Japanese friend is asking you what you've done. Your friend will ask about each item in the box. Tell him or her when you did the activity or when you plan to do it.

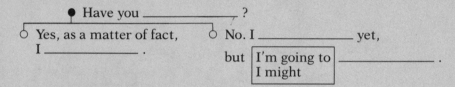

● *Have you been to the Tokyo National Museum?*
○ *Yes, as a matter of fact, I went there this morning. . . .*

> *Sushi* is small pieces of raw fish served on rice. *Kabuki* is a popular form of Japanese theater.

> take   took   taken

> The object pronoun for indefinite direct objects is *one*: see *a* tea ceremony ▶ see *one*.

Things to do	Done?	When?
1. go to the Tokyo National Museum	Yes	this morning
2. have sushi	No	tonight for dinner
3. take the bullet train	No	maybe tomorrow
4. see a tea ceremony	Yes	yesterday afternoon
5. go to the Tokyo Tower	Yes	two days ago
6. see a kabuki play	No	maybe tomorrow night

8 (MAKE SUGGESTIONS)

Now suggest doing each of the activities listed in exercise 7. Then make suggestions about places to visit in your town.

      ● Why don't you _____ ?
○ _____ .   ○ Good idea. _____ yet.
● You have? When _____ ? . . .

● *Why don't you go to the Tokyo National Museum?*
○ *I've already been there.*
● *You have? When did you go? . . .*

Can I let you know?

Laura is having a cup of coffee with her friend Wendy, who's from England. 📼

①

Wendy: Are you going out with Chuck tonight?
Laura: Uh-huh. He's supposed to pick me up at a quarter to seven. What time is it now?
Wendy: Half past six. You'd better get going.
Laura: You're kidding! I haven't even taken a shower.
Wendy: Where are you going?
Laura: We haven't made up our minds yet. Maybe to a movie, maybe to a party.
Wendy: Go and see *Tootsie*. It's supposed to be fantastic.
Laura: Oh, maybe we will. I've heard *Gandhi* is good, too.
Wendy: If you like long movies. Personally, I don't. Well, I really should be going. Do you want to go shopping tomorrow?
Laura: I'd like to, but it depends. I might have to go to the studio tomorrow and do some work. Can I let you know first thing in the morning?
Wendy: O.K. That would be all right. (*Rrring, rrring*)
Laura: Oh, there's the phone. It must be Chuck.
Wendy: Well, I'll be going. Ring me up tomorrow.
Laura: I will. Have a good evening.
Wendy: You too.

> Notice these expressions of Wendy's, which are typically British:
>
> half past six (six thirty)
> Ring me up. (Call me.)

2. Figure it out

Say *Right*, *Wrong*, or *I don't know*.

1. Laura and Chuck might go to a party.   *Right.*
2. Wendy has already seen *Tootsie*.
3. Wendy and Laura are thinking of going shopping tomorrow.
4. Laura is going to work tomorrow.
5. Laura hasn't seen *Gandhi*.
6. Wendy will probably see *Gandhi*.

3. Listen in 📼

Laura is talking on the phone with Chuck. Read the statement below. Then listen to her side of the conversation and choose *a*, *b*, or *c*.

Laura and Chuck are talking about _____ .
a. a movie
b. a class
c. a restaurant

23

Your turn

Read the poster about the Science Fiction Film Festival. Then discuss these questions in groups:

1. Have you ever seen a science fiction movie? Have you seen any of these movies?
2. Do you like science fiction films? Why or why not?
3. What kinds of movies do you like the most? Why?
4. Is there a movie that most of the people in your group have seen? What did you think of the movie?

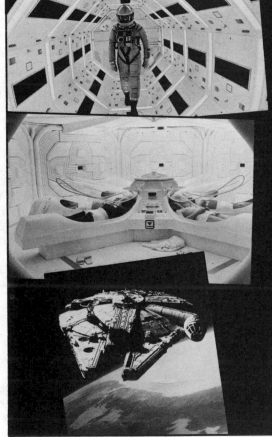

SCIENCE FICTION FILM FESTIVAL
MAY 16-18   RIVOLI THEATER

2001:
A SPACE ODYSSEY
(1968)

A computer named "Hal" tries to kill his programmers.
May 16 at 3:30, 6:30, and 9:30

ALIEN
(1979)

"Mother," the spaceship *Nostromo's* computer, wakes the crew from a deep sleep.
May 18 at 2:30, 5:30, and 8:30

Star Wars
(1977)

George Lucas directed this extremely imaginative film about war in outer space. Good guys, bad guys, and lots of fun.
May 17 at 1, 4, 7, and 10

Say it right

Say the words below. Then practice the conversations. 🔲

haven't [hǽvṇt]   hasn't [hǽzṇt]   doesn't [dǝ́zṇt]   didn't [dídṇt]   shouldn't [šúdṇt]

1. ● I haven't seen *E.T.* yet.
   ○ George hasn't either. Why don't you go with him?
   ● He doesn't want to see it.

2. ● I didn't call Nancy today. I didn't have time.
   ○ Well, we shouldn't call her now. It's after ten o'clock.

On your own

Read the article in *The Film Quarterly*. Then choose *a*, *b*, *c*, or *d*.

1. Spielberg's first films were _____ .
   a. comedies
   b. science fiction films
   c. horror films
   d. love stories

2. Spielberg does *not* like to _____ .
   a. talk with other film directors
   b. eat ice cream
   c. work long hours
   d. go to parties

3. After making a film, Spielberg feels _____ .
   a. happy
   b. depressed
   c. bored
   d. excited

4. Spielberg doesn't enjoy _____ .
   a. reading
   b. watching TV
   c. looking at films
   d. exercising

5. The Spielberg movie about a boy and girl in the desert is called _____ .
   a. *Star Wars*
   b. *Jaws*
   c. *Raiders of the Lost Ark*
   d. *Amblin'*

6. At parties Spielberg is usually _____ .
   a. outgoing
   b. friendly
   c. shy
   d. happy

Personality
of the month

Name: Steven Spielberg
Place of Birth: Cincinnati, Ohio
Occupation: Film director, producer, and writer
Most Famous Films: *Jaws* and *Jaws II* (1975 and 1978)
Close Encounters of the Third Kind (1977)
Raiders of the Lost Ark (1981)
E.T., The Extra-Terrestrial (1982)
Interests: Reading, studying films and television shows, and talking with other filmmakers
Dislikes: Parties—"When I go, I'm the guy in the corner. . . ."
Childhood Memories: Wanting to make films
Scaring his three sisters
Making horror movies starring his family
Comments: "Making movies is really all I know how to do." (Spielberg)
"He makes working fun." (Harrison Ford, the star of *Raiders of the Lost Ark*)
"His idea of exercise is to sit on the beach eating . . . while I run a mile." (Kathleen Carey, a friend)

Steven Spielberg is one of the most talented and successful filmmakers today. For Spielberg, success came early. When he was only twenty years old, he was given a seven-year contract with a movie studio after directing a twenty-two—minute movie called *Amblin'* about a boy and girl hitchhiking in the desert. He has made seven movies since he signed that contract, some of them the biggest moneymakers of recent years.

Spielberg's success did not come without hard work. When he's directing a film, he often works a hundred hours a week. When the film is finished, he gets depressed because he misses the people he worked with—people that Spielberg calls his "family."

Filmgoers all over the world have been thrilled by Spielberg's movies, and we are confident that he will make many more fantastic films in the future.

Words

I've heard it's . . .	think of	exhibit	get together	taken	a couple of
I've never heard of it.	the night before last	ceremony	thought	any good	latest
I'll let you know.	album	tower	might	a few of	
It's supposed to be.	circus	science fiction	decide		

4. What does the "K" stand for?

Try this

1. **Read the article and look at the table. Where were most of the immigrants to the United States from?**

2. **Are there immigrants in your country? If so, choose a partner and discuss these questions:**
   1. Where are they from?
   2. How long have they been in your country?
   3. Why did they come?
   4. What languages do they speak?

3. **Do you know any people from other countries who are living in your country? Tell the class about them.**
   1. What languages do they speak?
   2. Have they learned your language?

Immigration to the U.S.

Most U.S. citizens are either immigrants or descendants of immigrants.* More than fifty million (50,000,000) people have left the countries of their birth and come to the United States to live. Some came for excitement and adventure. Others came to escape poverty and hunger, or political and religious oppression. Still others were brought over from Africa as slaves. These immigrants have brought their customs, languages, and foods, and have made the United States a country of great ethnic and racial diversity.

*The only true nonimmigrants were the original inhabitants of the United States, the Native American Indians. Today they make up less than 1 percent of the population.

Country	1820–1979 total	Percent	Country	1820–1979 total	Percent
Europe	36,267,000	73.8	**America**	9,248,000	18.8
Germany	6,985,000	14.2	Canada	4,125,000	8.4
Italy	5,300,000	10.8	Mexico	2,177,000	4.4
Great Britain	4,914,000	10.0	West Indies	1,386,000*	2.7
Ireland	4,724,000	9.6	(includes Cuba and Haiti)		
Austria-Hungary	4,316,000	8.8			
The Soviet Union	3,376,000	6.9	**Africa**	142,000*	.3
Asia	3,038,000	6.2	**Australia and New Zealand**	123,000	.3
China	540,000	1.1			
The Philippines	431,000	.9	**All others**	309,000	.6
Japan	411,000	.8			
Turkey	386,000	.8			
Korea	276,000	.6			
Hong Kong	200,000	.4			

*These statistics do not include people of African descent who were brought over as slaves. By the time of the 1820 census, the slave trade was internal to the United States.

Luke Taylor and Maya Winston, two teachers at Bainridge High School, are talking about their families.

A ● Luke
   ○ Maya

- ● What an unusual necklace! What does the "K" stand for?
- ○ "Koziol." It's my maiden name.
- ● Oh, that's Polish, isn't it?
- ○ Yes. How did you know?
- ● My wife is Polish, and I've spent some time in Poland.
- ○ Oh, is that where you met?
- ● No, actually, we met here in the States. I was teaching English at the time, and she was one of my students.

B

○ Which language do you speak at home, English or Polish?

● English, most of the time. We used to speak more Polish before Stenia learned English so well.

○ She had a good teacher.

● Well, she worked really hard. In fact, she was one of my best students. She's also really good at languages.

○ What languages does she speak?

● Polish, Russian, French, and English. She speaks English almost perfectly now. She still has a very slight accent, but you can hardly tell she's foreign.

C

● Were either of your parents born in Poland?
○ Yes. They both were.
● Do they still speak Polish?
○ My father used to, but he doesn't anymore. He hasn't spoken it since my grandparents died. My mother doesn't speak a word.
● How long has she been in this country?

○ Since she was six. When she got here, she spoke Polish, Russian, and German fluently. Unfortunately, she forgot all of them as soon as she learned English.
● Do any of your relatives still live in Poland?
○ No. They all live here now. Most of them came over soon after my mother.

Figure it out

1. Say *Right, Wrong,* or *I don't know.*

1. Stenia and Luke sometimes speak Polish at home.   *Right.*
2. Koziol was Maya's name before she got married.
3. Stenia didn't know any English when she got to the U.S.
4. Stenia's grammar is excellent, but her accent is bad.
5. Maya's father still speaks Polish sometimes.
6. Maya's grandparents died a long time ago.

2. Match the words in italics with their meaning.

1. She worked *hard.*
2. Do they *still* speak Polish?
3. *Actually,* we met here.
4. *As soon as* she learned English, she forgot Polish.
5. She *hardly* speaks Polish.
6. He *used to* speak Polish, but he doesn't anymore.
7. *Unfortunately,* she's forgotten Polish.
8. We speak English *most of the time.*

a. It's too bad.
b. in the past
c. usually
d. now
e. a lot
f. very little
g. immediately after
h. as a matter of fact

Ways to say it

1 TALK ABOUT FOREIGN LANGUAGES

- What languages do you speak?
- ○ *French, Spanish, and (some) English.*
- Which one do you speak *the best*?
- ○ *French.*

> *Two* languages: Which one do you speak *better?*
> *Three or more* languages: Which one do you speak *the best?*

2 Close-up — *WHAT* VS. *WHICH*

What	languages	do you speak?
Which	language one	do you speak the best?

> Use *which* instead of *what* when referring to a definite group of alternatives:
>
> *What* languages do you speak (of all languages)?
> *Which* language (of the ones that you speak) do you speak the best?

3 Fill in the blanks with *what* or *which*.

1. ● I think I'll have soup. *What* kinds do you have?
   ○ Bean and onion. *Which* one would you like?
   ● Bean, please.

2. ● Excuse me— _____ way is the post office?
   ○ That way.
   ● And _____ time does it close?
   ○ At noon on Saturdays.

3. ● _____ sports do you like?
   ○ I like all sports.
   ● Yes, but _____ ones do you like the best?
   ○ Soccer and tennis.

4. ● _____ movies have you seen recently?
   ○ *Diva* and *Gandhi.*
   ● _____ one did you like better?
   ○ *Diva.*

4 TALK ABOUT FOREIGN LANGUAGES

- Do you speak *English* well?
- ○ *I hardly have an accent at all, but my grammar isn't very good.*

Do you speak English well?
I speak it quite well. (It's my native language.)
I speak it fluently, but I make mistakes.
I speak it correctly, but slowly.
I speak it very fast, but my accent is terrible.
I hardly have an accent at all, but my grammar isn't very good.
I understand it fairly well, but I speak it poorly.
I speak it very badly.

> I work very hard. = I do a lot of work.
> I hardly work at all. = I do almost no work.
> I hardly have an accent at all. = I have almost no accent.

5 Close-up — ADVERBS

Adjective	Adverb
correct perfect	correctly perfectly
terrible	terribly
easy	easily
fantastic	fantastically
slow fast hard	slow/slowly fast hard
good	well

> To form most adverbs, add *ly* to the adjective.
> If the adjective ends in *le,* change the *e* to *y.*
> If it ends in *y,* change the *y* to *i* and add *ly.* If it ends in *c,* add *ally.*

6 **Reword these evaluations of students using adverbs instead of adjectives.**

Donna speaks French quite well. . . .

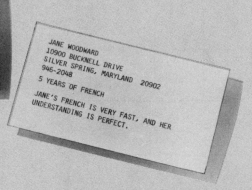

DONNA McBRIDE
1507 KORTH PLACE
SILVER SPRING, MARYLAND 20902
649-3422
5 YEARS OF FRENCH
DONNA'S FRENCH IS QUITE GOOD. IT'S
FLUENT AND USUALLY CORRECT.

GEORGE STONE
1203 CADDINGTON AVENUE
SILVER SPRING, MARYLAND 20901
593-1974
4 YEARS OF FRENCH
GEORGE'S FRENCH IS GOOD. IT'S SLOW,
BUT CORRECT.

JANE WOODWARD
10900 BUCKNELL DRIVE
SILVER SPRING, MARYLAND 20902
946-2048
5 YEARS OF FRENCH
JANE'S FRENCH IS VERY FAST, AND HER
UNDERSTANDING IS PERFECT.

7 (TALK ABOUT YOUR FAMILY)

● Was either of your parents born in another country?

○ Yes. My *mother* was. *She* was born in *Poland.*
● Does *she* still speak *Polish?*
○ *She used to, but she doesn't anymore.*
● How long has *she* been in this country?
○ Since *she was six years old.*

▲

| Since | 1918. |
| | she was six years old. |

○ Yes. | They both were. |
| | Both of them were. |

They were born in . . .

○ No. | They were both | born here. |
| | Both of them were |

Does she still speak Polish?

Yes. She speaks it most of the time.
Only occasionally—with a few friends.
She used to, but she doesn't anymore.
Not a word. Unfortunately, she's
  forgotten it completely.
No, not anymore. As soon as she came
  here, she stopped speaking it.

(forget
forgot
forgotten)

8

● Do any of your relatives live in another country?

○ Yes. *Some of them still* live in *Poland.*

○ No. | They all | live here. |
| | All of them |

9 (TELL HOW YOU MET SOMEONE)

● How did *you and your wife* meet?
○ *I was teaching English, and she was one of my students.*

How did you meet?
I was teaching English, and she was   one of my students. We had a mutual friend. We met at a party. We were living in the same building. We were going to the same school. We were working at the same place. We were taking the same course.

(She *was* teaching
English.
They *were* taking
  the same course.)

10 Close-up

PAST CONTINUOUS

Affirmative statements

I He She	was	teaching	English.
We You They	were		

Form past continuous negative statements, yes-no questions, and information questions the same way as for the present continuous, but use a *past* tense form of *be:*

I wasn't watching TV.
Were you eating dinner?
What were you doing?

11 ASK WHAT SOMETHING STANDS FOR

Use the words in the box to figure out what the initials stand for. If you have trouble, you may look up the answers on p. 134.

● What does *"U.N."* stand for?
○ (It stands for) *"United Nations."*

American	Soviet
Atlantic	Socialist
Nations	States
North	Treaty
Organization	Union
Republics	United

KEY VOTE TAKEN AT U.N.

O.A.S. Meets in Mexico City

NATO LEADERS CONFER IN BONN

U.S.S.R. says "Nyet"

NATO is pronounced [néytow].

12 TALK ABOUT EVENTS IN THE PAST

Read about Tullio Freitas, an immigrant to the United States. Then complete the sentences below, using *when, before, after, as soon as,* or *since* in your answers.

Tullio Freitas

I studied English in Brazil, but unfortunately I didn't study very hard. So when I came to the United States at the age of twenty-five, I hardly spoke any English at all.

At first I lived in a Portuguese neighborhood and spoke Portuguese most of the time. One day I was doing my laundry and I needed change. The only person in the laundromat was a young American woman. When I spoke to her in my broken English, she answered me in Portuguese. She was studying it at college.

Well, it was love at first sight. We got married two years later, and we've done our laundry together ever since. Now I speak English much better—almost as well as my five-year-old son.

1. Tullio studied English *before he came to the United States* .
2. He didn't know much English _____ .
3. He's learned most of his English _____ .
4. He spoke Portuguese most of the time _____ .
5. He and his wife got married two years _____ .
6. Tullio has been in the United States _____ .

I guess my mind was elsewhere.

Laura and Chuck are getting a bite to eat after seeing *Tootsie*.

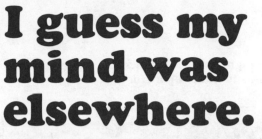

1

Laura: What a great movie! Wasn't it funny when he was baby-sitting?
Chuck: Hmm . . . I don't remember that part.
Laura: It was one of the funniest parts of the movie!
Chuck: I guess my mind was elsewhere.
Laura: You were thinking about the interview again, weren't you?
Chuck: I just can't seem to get it out of my mind. I really want that job, Laura.
Laura: I know you do.
Chuck: Mr. Dow seemed to think I was qualified. I can't figure out why I haven't heard yet. It's been nearly two weeks since I had the interview.
Laura: Well, they said it would be about ten days. Listen, if you're so anxious to find out, why don't you call them and ask if they've made a decision yet?
Chuck: Oh, I'm sure they'll let everyone know as soon as they've decided.
Laura: Well, relax then. Let's think about what we're going to order. What's good here?
Chuck: They used to have this great onion soup, but I don't see it anywhere on the menu.
Laura: Maybe they don't serve it anymore. Here comes the waiter. Let's ask him.

2. Figure it out

1. Say *Right, Wrong,* or *I don't know.*

1. Chuck had a job interview almost two weeks ago. *Right.*
2. Someone else got the job.
3. Chuck watched the movie very carefully.
4. Laura enjoyed the movie.
5. Chuck is unemployed.
6. Chuck has been to the restaurant before.

3. Listen in

The waiter is taking Laura and Chuck's order. Read the statements below. Then listen to the conversation and choose *a* or *b.*

1. The restaurant might be out of _____ .
   a. onion soup
   b. chicken soup
2. The last time Chuck ate at the restaurant
   _____ .

   a. the waiter was already working there
   b. the waiter wasn't working there yet

Your turn

Karin Meyer came to the United States from Germany in 1947. Here's a page from her scrapbook. What do you think happened in her life between 1944 and 1947? Work in groups to make up a story.

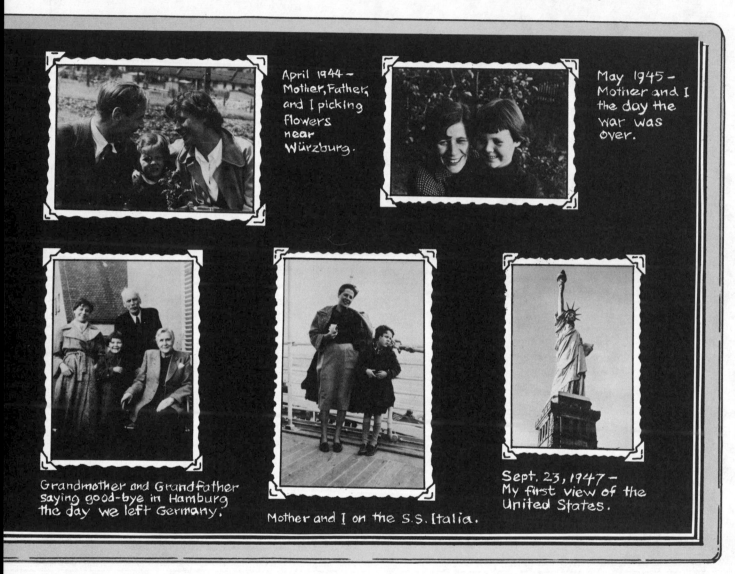

April 1944 – Mother, Father, and I picking flowers near Würzburg.

May 1945 – Mother and I the day the war was over.

Grandmother and Grandfather saying good-bye in Hamburg the day we left Germany.

Mother and I on the S.S. Italia.

Sept. 23, 1947 – My first view of the United States.

On your own

Read the description of the lecture series at the Ridgefield Museum of Natural History. Then imagine that you went to all three lectures. Which lecture did each of these quotations come from—lecture #1, lecture #2, or lecture #3?

1. "The first immigrants to the Americas traveled very slowly and followed the rivers."
   lecture #2
2. "The people had a difficult life, but they were generally healthy."
3. "Some scientists say there is evidence that the immigrants came twenty-five thousand years ago."
4. "The people moved from North America to South America."
5. "The immigrants lived in groups of about fifty."
6. "Thousands of years ago a land bridge connected Asia and North America."
7. "The first Native Americans probably hunted with dogs."

Ancient Immigrants

Weekends in July

When Europeans first crossed the Atlantic Ocean and came to the New World, there were hundreds of thousands of Native Americans living there. Where did these people come from? How did they live? During the month of July, the Ridgefield Museum of Natural History will present a series of lectures that will answer some of these questions.

<u>Lecture #1</u>   Saturday, July 9   1 PM
                 Sunday, July 10   3 PM
This lecture will explore when the first people arrived from Asia. Although most archeologists agree that there were people living in North America twelve thousand years ago, there are some who believe that the first groups arrived much earlier—twenty or even thirty thousand years before that. Yet some other scholars believe that they arrived later than twelve thousand years ago. The first lecture will give evidence for these different views and explain how archeologists date their findings.

<u>Lecture #2</u>   Saturday, July 16   1 PM
                 Sunday, July 17   3 PM
The second lecture will discuss the important part geography played in the movement of these ancient people. The lecturers will explain why archeologists believe that a land bridge used to connect Asia and North America. They will also show how the position of mountains and rivers influenced the routes that the first immigrants chose.

<u>Lecture #3</u>   Saturday, July 23   1 PM
                 Sunday, July 24   3 PM
The daily life of these early immigrants will be the subject of the final lecture. The lecturers will explain how the immigrants lived in such a difficult climate, how they made clothes, and how they hunted and killed large animals. There will also be an exhibit of ancient tools which archeologists have found.

Words

immigrant	bean	not . . . anymore	as soon as	fluently	perfectly
accent	stand for	either of	best	fairly	unfortunately
grammar	get married	any of	mutual	recently	completely
mistake	forgotten	hardly	native	correctly	occasionally
relative	(forget)	at all	quite	poorly	

5. You can't miss it.

Try this

1. **Read the reviews of three Toronto restaurants. Then choose a partner and compare the restaurants to each other.**

   You may use these adjectives: *expensive, reasonable, cheap, relaxed,* and *lively.*

2. **Now make plans with three other students to have dinner out in your town. Compare different restaurants and then decide where to go.**

   Here are some more adjectives you may use: *close, far,* small, large, crowded,* and *busy.*

3. **Using the map below, give another student directions to Toby's "Good Eats." You're on Hazelton.**

   *The comparative form of *far* is *farther.*

Two tourists, Kathy and George Dupont, are looking for a place to have lunch in Toronto. 🔲

A
- ● Kathy
- ○ Man in street
- ▲ George

● Excuse me, sir . . . we're looking for a place to have lunch. Do you know of any restaurants around here?

○ Well, there are quite a few. Did you have anything special in mind?

▲ Oh, just someplace reasonable with good food.

○ Well, you know, this is one of the most expensive areas in town.

● Can you recommend a place that's not too expensive?

○ Let's see now. . . . The closest place that I can think of offhand is Toby's. It's supposed to be reasonable, and everyone says the food is good. They serve all kinds of hamburgers.

▲ That sounds fine.

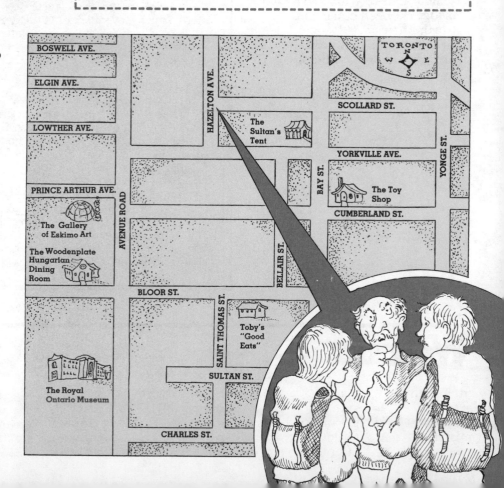

B

▲ Could you tell us how to get to the restaurant?
○ Do you know where Yorkville Avenue is?
▲ Yes.
○ Well, when you get to Yorkville, turn left. Then go one more block and turn right on Bellair. Just stay on Bellair until you get to Bloor Street. The restaurant will be right across the street. You can't miss it.
● What's it called again?
○ Toby's "Good Eats."

C

● One more thing . . . what's the best way to get to the Art Gallery of Ontario?
○ You can either walk or take the subway.
▲ How far is it? My feet are killing me.
○ Oh, not that far. About a thirty-minute walk, I'd say.
▲ We'll take the subway.
○ Well, then after you eat, walk a couple of blocks west on Bloor and take the University subway south to St. Patrick.
● Thanks a lot. You've been very helpful.
○ Don't mention it. Enjoy your day.

Figure it out

1. Say *Right*, *Wrong*, or *I don't know*.

1. George and Kathy don't want to spend a lot of money.   *Right.*
2. The man has eaten at Toby's many times.
3. George's feet hurt.

4. Most of the restaurants in the area are very reasonable.
5. George and Kathy are going to take the subway to the restaurant.
6. George and Kathy have been to Toronto before.

2. Choose *a* or *b*.

1. Do you know _____ ?
   a. where is Bloor Street
   b. where Bloor Street is

2. Could you tell us how _____ ?
   a. to get there
   b. do you get there

3. It's a _____ walk.
   a. ten-minutes
   b. ten-minute

4. Stay on Bellair until _____ .
   a. you'll get to Bloor
   b. you get to Bloor

Ways to say it

1 ASK FOR ADVICE

● Do you know of any *hotels* around here?

○ Yes, there's one on *State Street*.

○ Well, there are quite a few. Did you have anything special in mind?

 ● Oh, someplace *clean and inexpensive*.

○ No, I'm afraid I don't.

a hotel	a restaurant
clean	reasonable
inexpensive	unusual
convenient	close
modern	with good food
with parking	with a nice
	atmosphere
	with fast service

2 Close-up

INDEFINITE COMPOUNDS WITH ADJECTIVES

someone	anyone	no one	everyone
something	anything	nothing	everything
someplace	anyplace	no place	everyplace
somewhere	anywhere	nowhere	everywhere

someone important
anywhere interesting
nothing special
everything good

3 Fill in each blank with an indefinite compound followed by an adjective when appropriate.

● Hi, dear. How was your day? Did you do _anything_ _special_?

○ No, _____ _____ .

● Well, did you go _____ ?

○ No, _____ _____ .

● I see you're reading the TV section. Is there _____ _____ on TV?

○ _____ _____ . Just the same old shows. I've already seen _____ _____ .

● Oh, by the way, did _____ call?

○ No, _____ _____ . Just your mother.

4 ASK FOR ADVICE

● Can you recommend a *nice restaurant* (in this neighborhood)?

○ Yes. I know of one.
● Is *it expensive?* . . .

○ Well, there are *three— The Harvest, The Kitchen,* and *Silvia's.*
● Which one is *the nicest?*
○ *The Harvest is the nicest, but it's also the most expensive.* . . .

○ No, I'm sorry, I don't know of any.

Two restaurants: The Harvest is *nicer than* The Kitchen.
Three or more restaurants: The Harvest is *the nicest* restaurant.

▼

Can you recommend. . . ?	
a nice restaurant	a good shoe store
a good doctor	a clothing store
a dentist	a bakery

Some adjectives
nice
close
far
good
expensive
inexpensive

Which one is . . . ?	
nicer	the nicest
closer	the closest
farther	the farthest
better	the best
more expensive	the most expensive
less expensive	the least expensive

5 ASK HOW TO GET SOMEWHERE

Ask how to get to one of the places you talked about in exercise 4.

- What's the best way to get / How do you get to *The Harvest?*
- ○ You can either *walk* or *take a bus.*
- How far is it?
- ○ Oh, it's about *a thirty-minute walk* or *fifteen minutes by bus.*

Some means of transportation	Some times
walk	a thirty-minute walk
take a bus	a fifteen-minute bus (subway) ride
take a subway	ten minutes by subway (bus)
drive	a two-hour drive

thirty minutes, *but* a thirty-minute walk

---

6 Close-up

THE SUPERLATIVE OF ADJECTIVES

Silvia's has	the	fastest	service in town.
The Harvest is		most expensive	restaurant.

One syllable or ending in *y*	More than one syllable
adjective + *est*	*most* or *least* + adjective

Before adding *er* or *est*:
Drop the *e* when an adjective ends in *e*.
Double the consonant when an adjective ends in a single vowel + a consonant.
Change *y* to *i*.

Adjective	Comparative form	Superlative form
fast	faster	the fastest
close	closer	the closest
big	bigger	the biggest
busy	busier	the busiest
good	better	the best
bad	worse	the worst
far	farther	the farthest
expensive	more expensive	the most expensive
inexpensive	less expensive	the least expensive

---

7 Complete the letter. Fill in each blank with the comparative or superlative form of the adjective given.

Dear Mary and Bob,   December 20, 1984

busy — I'm really sorry I haven't written, but the holidays are
the busiest time of year for me at the store.
big — The children are a lot _____ than when you saw them.
tall — I think Jim is going to be _____ one in the family very
good — soon. Nancy is one of _____ students in her class. She
had a little trouble with math last year, but it's a lot
easy — _____ for her now.
happy — Harry is _____ and _____ since he started his new
important — job. _____ thing is that the hours are _____.
bad — This has been one of the _____ winters in a long
warm — time. I hope the weather gets _____.
How's everything with you?

relaxed
short

37

8 ASK FOR DIRECTIONS

You're at the corner of Hazelton and Scollard in Toronto. Ask how to get to one of the places listed in the box. Another student will give you directions using the map on p. 34. Take notes if necessary.

- Could you please tell me how to get to *Toby's "Good Eats"?*
- ○ Sure. Do you know where Yorkville Avenue is?
- Yes, I do.
- ○ Well, when you get to Yorkville, turn *left. Then go one more block and turn right on Bellair. Stay on Bellair until you get to Bloor Street. Toby's will be right across the street.* You can't miss it.
- Thanks a lot. You've been very helpful.
- ○ Don't mention it.

Some places in Toronto
Toby's "Good Eats"
The Sultan's Tent
The Toy Shop
The Gallery of Eskimo Art
The Woodenplate Hungarian Dining Room
The Royal Ontario Museum

Some locations
across the street
on the left
about halfway down the block
on the corner

Compare:
Where's Yorkville Avenue?
Do you know where Yorkville Avenue is?

9 Close-up

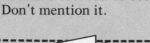

TIME CLAUSES WITH *WHEN, JUST BEFORE, JUST AFTER, AS SOON AS,* AND *UNTIL*

	when	
Turn right	just before	
You'll see the store	just after	you get to Bloor.
	as soon as	
Stay on Bellair	until	

Always use a present tense verb in time clauses that refer to future time, even when another verb in the sentence is in the future:

Turn right when you *get* to Bloor.
You'll pass two traffic lights before you *get* there.

10

You're walking on First Street when a driver stops you and asks for directions. Complete the conversation with appropriate time clauses using the map on the right.

- Excuse me—how do you get to Mama's Kitchen from here?
- ○ Stay on First Street <u>*until you get to*</u> Market Street. _____ Market, turn right. Then go straight ahead _____ Baker Street. _____ Baker, you'll see a big church. _____ the church, get in the left lane. Turn left on Baker at the light. The restaurant is about halfway down the block on the left.

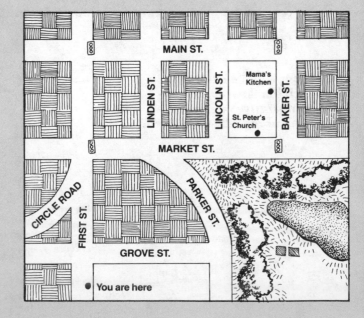

You can't keep them home anymore.

Laura's mother, Mrs. Enders, is shopping for a gift for Laura's sister at a neighborhood store.

1

Saleswoman:	May I help you find something, or are you just looking?
Mrs. Enders:	I'm trying to find something for my daughter. She just moved into a new apartment.
Saleswoman:	Did you have anything special in mind?
Mrs. Enders:	Something practical. I know she needs a lot of things. . . . Maybe a nice pot.
Saleswoman:	Well, these are the best pots we carry. Feel how heavy this one is.
Mrs. Enders:	I'm afraid it's a bit too heavy. I have to carry it with me on the plane.
Saleswoman:	Well, they also come in smaller sizes. I've had some since I got married, and they're still like new.
Mrs. Enders:	I'll take this smaller one. Do you accept credit cards?
Saleswoman:	No, I'm sorry, we don't. We take either cash or a check. Where does your daughter live?
Mrs. Enders:	In Chicago. As a matter of fact, both of my daughters live in Chicago. You know kids nowadays. They like the excitement of the big cities.
Saleswoman:	It's true. You can't keep them home anymore. My son is thinking of moving to Chicago. He had an interview there. Now he's waiting to hear if he got the job.
Mrs. Enders:	Who do I make the check out to?
Saleswoman:	Lee's Kitchen Shop.

2. Figure it out

Say *Right*, *Wrong*, or *I don't know*.

1. Mrs. Enders is going to Chicago.   *Right.*
2. The saleswoman's son is moving to Chicago.
3. Laura's sister is looking for an apartment.
4. Mrs. Enders buys the heaviest pot.
5. Mrs. Enders has two daughters.
6. Mrs. Enders gives the saleswoman cash.

3. Listen in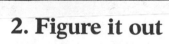

Mrs. Enders also needs a bathroom scale. Read the statement below. Then listen to the conversation and choose *a* or *b*.

Ace Hardware is _____.
a. before The Shoe Place
b. after The Shoe Place

39

Your turn

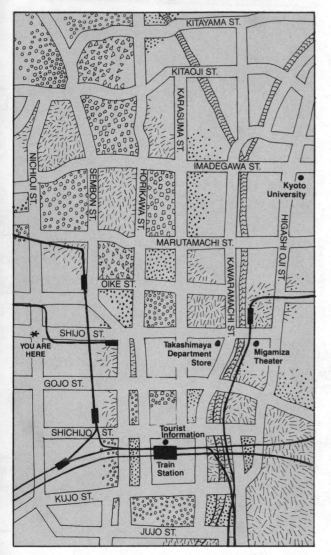

Imagine that you live in Kyoto, Japan. Your partner is a tourist who starts a conversation with you and then asks you one of the questions below. Using the map, give your partner directions to the appropriate place. You are standing on the corner of Nichioji Street and Shijo Street.

1. Where can I get a train to Tokyo?
2. Where can I get some information about Kyoto?
3. Where can I buy some presents for my family?
4. I'd like to see a Japanese play. Is there a theater near here?
5. My cousin teaches at Kyoto University, and I'd like to see the school. Is it far from here?

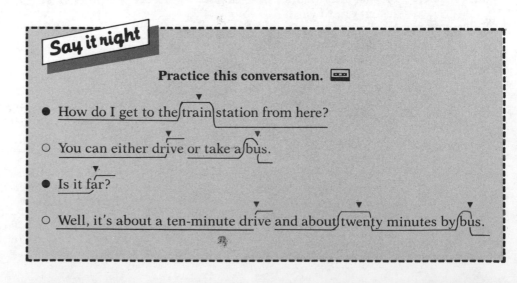

Say it right

Practice this conversation. 📼

● How do I get to the train station from here?

○ You can either drive or take a bus.

● Is it far?

○ Well, it's about a ten-minute drive and about twenty minutes by bus.

40

On your own

Read the newspaper article. Then say *Right* or *Wrong*.

1. The Disney parks in the United States were cheaper to build than the one in Japan.   *Right.*
2. Japanese Disneyland is not as large as Walt Disney World.
3. Walt Disney built Japanese Disneyland.
4. Japanese Disneyland is an example of American influence in Japan.
5. Japan has influenced business in the United States.
6. There are only a few Japanese radios and televisions in the United States.
7. You can see a show called "The Eternal Sea" at all of the Disney parks.

A Bridge Between the U.S. and Japan

Walking down the street in many cities or towns in the United States, you can see the influence of Japan. Many people watch Japanese televisions, listen to Japanese radios, and drive Japanese cars. Some even work in Japanese companies. It is no longer unusual for U.S. companies to invite Japanese experts to the United States to offer business advice. Japanese restaurants are now so popular that most people have heard of sushi, even if they are afraid to try it.

Meanwhile, back in Japan the world's largest Disneyland opened recently near Tokyo. Mickey Mouse was there to welcome visitors, and so were Minnie Mouse, Donald Duck, Dumbo the Elephant, and all of Walt Disney's other famous characters.

Oriental Land Company, the Japanese company that owns and built the park, began work more than twenty years ago. Today the finished Disneyland covers 202 acres, 114 of these actual park space. The original Disneyland, the famous amusement center near Los Angeles created by Walt Disney in 1955, has only 74 acres of park space. Walt Disney World in Florida has 106. Not only is Japanese Disneyland the largest Disney park, it was also the most expensive to create. It cost over 652 million dollars to build, not including the price of the land.

The park is a prime example of Japanese-American cooperation. Oriental Land Company received advice from Walt Disney Productions in California during construction. In return, the American company will share the money that the park earns. The mixing of two cultures can be seen throughout the park. Restaurants sell sushi, along with hamburgers, hot dogs, and French fries. All signs are in Japanese and English. Side by side with the famous Disney characters are two shows of special interest to the Japanese. "Meet the World" presents over 2,000 years of Japanese history, and "The Eternal Sea" takes viewers to the bottom of the sea around Japan.

The park has been extremely popular, and Masatomo Takahashi, the head of Oriental Land Company, is proud of his new Disneyland. "The park," he says, "should be another bridge for understanding between the U.S. and Japan."

Words

See p. 36 for a list of indefinite compounds and p. 37 for a list of superlative forms of adjectives.

know of	bakery	neighborhood	church	either . . . or	special
have something in mind	clothing store	atmosphere	recommend	reasonable	helpful
I'm afraid I don't.	shoe store	present (n)	just before	unusual	relaxed
Don't mention it.	section	information	just after	modern	lively
You can't miss it.	show (n)	lane	halfway	inexpensive	

For **Mrs. Clark**

Date **10/14** Time **2:00**

WHILE YOU WERE OUT

Mr. **John Willard**

From **The Wheaton Company**

Phone No. **687-3456**

☑ TELEPHONED   ☑ URGENT
☑ PLEASE CALL   ☐ WANTS TO SEE YOU
☐ WILL CALL AGAIN   ☐ CAME TO SEE YOU
☐ RETURNED YOUR CALL

Message **He'll be out from 2:30 to 3:00.**

Try this

Read the message form. Then choose a partner and act out these two conversations. Play the role of John Willard or Anne Jenkins. End the second conversation any way you wish.

1. John Willard calls Joan Clark, the president of Clark Associates, at 2:00. Mrs. Clark is at a meeting. Her assistant, Anne Jenkins, takes the message on the message form.

2. At 4:30 Mr. Willard calls again because Mrs. Clark hasn't called back. Mrs. Clark just got back, and Mrs. Jenkins gave her the message as soon as she came in.

It's a busy day for Anne Jenkins, an administrative assistant at Clark Associates. 🔲

A
  ● Joan Clark
  ○ Anne Jenkins

● Anne, do you know what time it is?
○ It's ten to twelve.
● Listen, would you do me a favor? I have a meeting with Alex Post, and I'm supposed to be there at noon. Would you call him for me and tell him I'm on my way?
○ Sure.
● Thanks a lot. Oh, and one more thing . . . if my son Johnny calls, tell him to be ready at six. I'll pick him up on my way home.
○ O.K.

● Oh, wait, I'd better call my husband. He might think *he's* supposed to pick up Johnny.
○ Why don't you just go? I'll call him for you.
● Do you mind?
○ No, not at all.
● Thanks so much. By the way, did you send Mr. Post our sales report?
○ Yes. I sent it to him last week.
● I can always count on you, Anne. Well, I'm off. I should be back no later than three.

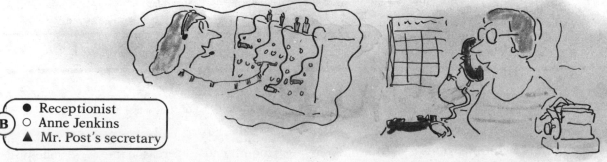

B
  ● Receptionist
  ○ Anne Jenkins
  ▲ Mr. Post's secretary

● Post, Cramden, and Lowe.
○ Alex Post, please. (*Rrring, rrring*)
▲ Mr. Post's office.

○ May I speak to Mr. Post, please?
▲ May I tell him who's calling?
○ Yes, this is Anne Jenkins from Clark Associates.

at time it is?

C
○ Anne Jenkins
● Donald Todd
▲ Office worker

○ Good afternoon, Clark Associates.
● May I please speak to Mrs. Clark?
○ I'm sorry, she's not in the office.
● When do you expect her back?
○ She should be back by three. Would you like to leave a message?
● This is Donald Todd. Would you please have her call me? My number is 666-4433. It's quite important.

○ I'll give her the message as soon as she gets in.
● Thank you.
▲ Uh . . . excuse me, can I ask you a question? Could you show me how to work the photocopier? I'm not sure where to put the paper.
○ Sure, I'd be glad to.
▲ Maybe you could explain the instructions to me. I can't seem to figure them out.

D
● Joan Clark
○ Anne Jenkins

● Well, see you tomorrow.
○ I'd better go, too. Thursday's my daughter's birthday, and I want to get her a new robe.
● I think you're going to have to buy it for her tomorrow. The stores are closing in fifteen minutes.
○ Oh, no! You're right. I guess I lost track of the time.

Figure it out

1. Say *Right, Wrong,* or *I don't know.*

1. Mrs. Clark is going to be late to her meeting. *Right.*
2. Mrs. Clark's son might call.
3. Mrs. Jenkins is going to tell Mr. Clark to pick Johnny up.
4. Donald Todd called before three.
5. Mrs. Jenkins has worked at Clark Associates for a long time.
6. Mrs. Jenkins always knows what time it is.

2. Match.

1. Would you please have her
2. Tell my son
3. I gave it
4. I'm not sure where
5. I bought it
6. He explained
7. He asked

a. me that question.
b. for you.
c. call me.
d. to you.
e. that question to me.
f. to put the paper.
g. do I put the paper.
h. to call me.

43

Ways to say it

1 EXPRESS AN OBLIGATION

- Do you know what time it is?
- ○ (It's) *ten to twelve.*
- Oh, I'd better go. I'm supposed to *be at a meeting* at *noon.*

> I'd better . . . =
> I had better . . .

Time now	Obligation
11:50	be at a meeting at 12:00
12:25	meet Joe for lunch at 12:30
2:35	pick up the children at 3:00
3:50	be back at the office at 4:00

> *I have to* and *I'm supposed to* both express obligation, but use *I'm supposed to* when you might not (or can't) meet the obligation. Compare:
>
> I have to go to a meeting (so I'm going).
> I'm supposed to go to a meeting (but I might not go).
> I'm supposed to be in class right now (but I'm not).
> I'm supposed to go to a movie later (but I might change my plans).

> Noun objects of two-word verbs may be placed between or after the two words. Pronoun objects are placed between the two words:
>
> Pick the children up.
> Pick up the children. ▶ Pick them up.

2 ASK A FAVOR OF SOMEONE

- Would you do me a favor?

  Would you | *send this report to Alex Post?*
  send Alex Post this report?

- ○ Sure.

> These indirect objects with *for* act like indirect objects with *to:*
>
> Buy a copy of *Time* for me. =
> Buy me a copy of *Time.*

> The indirect object must follow the direct object of *explain,* but must precede the direct object of *ask.*

Some favors

Send this report to Alex Post.
Give this note to Meg when you see her.
Lend your book to me when you're done with it.

Buy a copy of *Time* for me when you go out.
Get a newspaper for me on your way home.
Make an appointment for me with Dr. Janik.

Explain the homework to me.
Ask Don his new phone number.

3 MAKE A REQUEST

- *I can't seem to figure out these instructions.* Could you *explain them to me?*
- ○ Sure. (I'd be glad to.)

Some situations	Some requests
I can't seem to figure out these instructions.	Introduce me to him.
	Explain them to me.
I borrowed these books from your wife.	Send it to him.
I'd like to meet your friend Bill.	Give them back to her.
Mr. Post would like to see our sales report.	Buy one for me.
I forgot to get a newspaper.	

4 Close-up

DIRECT AND INDIRECT OBJECTS

Indirect objects with *to* and *for*

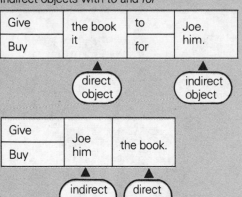

Give	the book	to	Joe.
Buy	it	for	him.

direct object — indirect object

Give	Joe	the book.
Buy	him	

indirect object — direct object

Use *to* before the indirect object with these verbs:

bring	sell	take
give	send	tell
lend	show	

Use *for* before the indirect object with these verbs:

bake	find	save
build	get	
buy	make	

When the direct object is a pronoun, the indirect object follows it.

To + the indirect object always comes *after* the direct object of these verbs:

describe	introduce	say
explain	return	

Explain the instructions to me.

The indirect object always comes *before* the direct object of the verb *ask*:

He asked me a question.

---

5 Fill in each blank with a direct and an indirect object pronoun. When the direct object is a noun, it is given in parentheses.

1. ● Tomorrow is Julie's birthday.
   ○ Really? Is someone going to bake
   <u>*her a cake*</u> ? (cake)
   ● No, but Paul bought _____ . (big chocolate cake)   It looks delicious.

2. ● I borrowed this book from Sally two weeks ago. I really have to return _____ .
   ○ I'm going to see her later. I can give _____ then.

3. ● Why are you talking in class, Johnny?
   ○ Pete asked _____ . (question)   He didn't understand the math problem.
   ● I'll explain _____ after class, Pete. Please sit quietly.

4. ● Have you called my uncle, Tim? Maybe he can find _____ . (job)
   ○ No, not yet. I know I should.
   ● Well, actually, he's coming over for dinner tomorrow. I'll introduce _____ then.

---

6 OFFER TO DO SOMEONE A FAVOR

● I'd better *call Evelyn Roche. She's expecting me in five minutes.*

○ Oh, I'll | *call her* / do it | for you.

> In the sentence *I'll call her for you,* for does not introduce an indirect object.

I'd better . . .	Reason
call Evelyn Roche.	I need my suit tonight.
type these letters.	She's expecting me in five minutes.
copy this report.	I don't have time to take the bus.
pick up the dry cleaning.	They have to go out today.
call a taxi.	Mr. Garcia will want a copy.

---

7 LEAVE A MESSAGE WITH SOMEONE

● I'm leaving now, *Anne.* If *my son* calls, tell *him to be ready at six.*

○ O.K. What time will you be back?

● Oh, I should be back by *three.*

> *by* = *no later than*

Some people	Some messages
my son	Tell her I'll call her back after dinner.
the travel agent	Tell him to be ready at six.
Mary Fox	Tell her I'll pick up the tickets tomorrow.
the repairman	Tell him to come fix the typewriter as soon as he can.

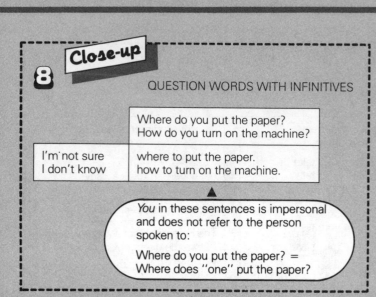

8 Close-up

QUESTION WORDS WITH INFINITIVES

	Where do you put the paper? How do you turn on the machine?
I'm not sure I don't know	where to put the paper. how to turn on the machine.

▲

You in these sentences is impersonal and does not refer to the person spoken to:

Where do you put the paper? =
Where does "one" put the paper?

9 ASK FOR HELP

● Could you show me how to *work the photocopier?* I'm not sure *where* to *put the paper.*

○ Sure, I'd be glad to. ○ I'm not really sure how to *work it* either.

How do you . . . ?	Some specific questions
work the photocopier use the washing machine fill out this form use the telephone use the tape recorder	How do you turn down the volume? Where do you put the paper? When do you dial the number? What do you write on this line? Where do you put the detergent?

10 CALL AN OFFICE

| Mrs. Clark | Mr. Apple | Miss Chu | Mr. Kent | Mr. Benowitz | Mrs. Branch |

● Clark Associates.
○ May I speak to *Mrs. Clark,* please?

● May I tell *her* who's calling?
○ Yes, this is *Donald Todd.*
● Just one moment, please.

● I'm sorry. *She*'s not in the office *right now.*
○ When do you expect *her* back?
● *She* should be back *by three.* Would you like to leave a message?
○ Yes. Would you have *her* call me when *she* gets back? My name is *Donald Todd* and my number is *666-4433.*
● I'll give *her* the message as soon as *she* comes back, *Mr. Todd.*

Information for the secretary
Mrs. Clark is supposed to be back by three. Mr. Apple just stepped out for a few minutes. Miss Chu is on vacation until next Monday. Mr. Kent is out to lunch until two. Mr. Benowitz and Mrs. Branch are in.

Ways you've said it
Could you ask her to call me?

I was starting to worry.

Back in Columbus, Ohio, Doug is eating dinner with his family.

1

Doug: Does anyone know what time it is?
Father: It's exactly seven o'clock.
Doug: I've got to get going soon. Someone's supposed to come over at eight to look at the apartment.
Mother: Well, you can't leave before you have a piece of this cake Dad made.
Doug: Hey, chocolate cake! All right!
Father: It's in honor of your new job.
Doug: You know, I still can't believe I got it. I was starting to worry when two weeks went by with no news.
Father: Well, you know what they say, "No news is good news."
Doug: Hey, Ricky, how would you like to do your favorite brother a big favor? Could you and some of your friends give me a hand packing on Saturday?
Ricky: Sure, I guess so.
Doug: Thanks, Ricky. You're a great brother.

2. Listen in

Meanwhile, in Chicago Carlos, one of Laura's coworkers, gives her a telephone message. Read the statements below. Then listen to the conversation and choose *a* or *b*.

1. Chuck wants Laura _____ .
   a. to call him back
   b. to meet him after work

2. Laura is expecting Jack Thomson _____ .
   a. to call her
   b. to come to the office

3

Laura dials Chuck's number.

Chuck: Hello?
Laura: Hi, Chuck. You sound a little down. Is anything wrong?
Chuck: Remember I was starting to worry when I hadn't heard anything in two weeks? Well, today I got a call. . . .

4. Figure it out

Say *Right*, *Wrong*, or *I don't know*.

1. Doug is going to move to Chicago. *Right*.
2. Doug has already found an apartment in Chicago.
3. Doug is expecting someone at his apartment.
4. Ricky and his friends are going to help Doug.
5. Doug and Chuck probably applied for the same job.

Your turn

Laura Monteverdi is a very rich woman who lives at the Westminster Arms Hotel in London. She just received this letter saying that someone has kidnapped her dog, Zefira. Read the letter very carefully. The police think that one of the people below kidnapped Zefira. Read the descriptions, and study the letter again. Work in groups to figure out which person is the kidnapper.

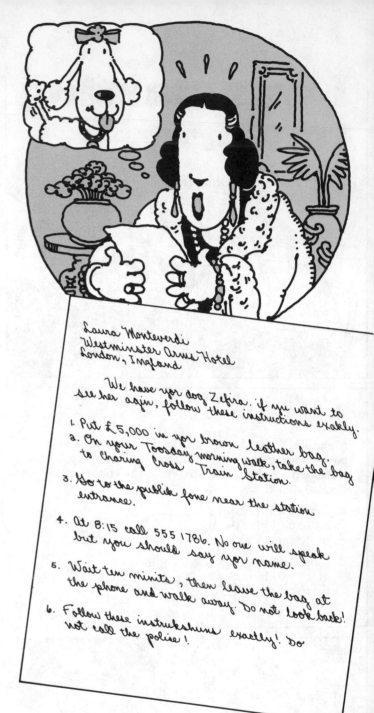

Alexandra Pavlova is visiting Mrs. Monteverdi. She just arrived from Moscow three days ago. She hasn't seen Mrs. Monteverdi in fifteen years.

Rudolfo Bellini gives piano lessons to Mrs. Monteverdi's daughter. He has come to the house three times a week for three years. The police tried to ask him some questions, but he couldn't help them because he only speaks Italian.

Hilary Harper is Mrs. Monteverdi's secretary. She left London yesterday after she received a telegram saying that her mother was very sick. The police would like to question her and hope she will return soon.

Brian Butterworth is Mrs. Monteverdi's driver, and he has worked for her family since he left school at the age of fifteen. Mrs. Monteverdi told the police that she is sure he didn't kidnap Zefira.

Laura Monteverdi
Westminster Arms Hotel
London, England

We have yor dog Zefira. if you want to see her agin, follow these instructions exakly.

1. Put £5,000 in yor brown leather bag.
2. On your Toosday morning walk, take the bag to Charing Cross Train Station.
3. Go to the publik fone near the station entrance.
4. At 8:15 call 555 1786. No one will speak but you should say yor name.
5. Wait ten minits, then leave the bag at the phone and walk away. Do not look back!
6. Follow these instrukshuns exactly! Do not call the polise!

48

On your own

What does your handwriting say about you?

People have been fascinated by handwriting for a long time. The first book on graphology, the study of handwriting, was written in 1632, and since that time hundreds of books have been published on the subject.

Graphologists believe that you can learn a lot about people's personalities by looking at the way they write. Some of the characteristics they look at are slant—whether your letters point forward or backward, pressure—whether you press hard or only lightly on the paper, and the size of capital letters. As shown below, each of these characteristics can reveal different personality tendencies. For example, if you slant your letters forward, you are probably an outgoing, friendly person.

SLANT	TENDENCY
forward	an outgoing, friendly person
up and down	a logical person
backward	a person with many secrets
PRESSURE	
heavy	a very emotional person
light	an impractical person
CAPITAL LETTERS	
Fancy	a vain person
Large	a confident person
Small	a shy person
Typical	an unimaginative person

Graphologists also look at which parts of the letters seem larger or more important. For this purpose they have divided the letters into three zones or areas.

defghijklmn — upper / middle / lower

According to one graphologist, if the part of the letter in the upper zone is very large compared to the part in the middle zone, then the writer is probably idealistic. If the part in the lower zone is very large, it shows that the writer is very interested in money and success. If the letters of all the zones are well balanced, the writer is probably practical.

Whether or not you close letters such as _a_ or _o_ also says something about your personality.

open — If the letters _a_ or _o_ are open, the writer is probably an honest person who likes to talk.

closed — If these letters are closed, the writer is good at keeping a secret.

The police have asked graphologists to help them solve crimes, and businesses have used handwriting samples to choose employees. So the next time you sit down to write a letter, fill out a form, or even write your name—be careful. You may be telling people more than you think.

Read the magazine article. Then say _Right_ or _Wrong_.

1. The way you write can tell a graphologist about your personality.   _Right._
2. People have studied handwriting for more than 350 years.
3. Emotional people press very hard when they write.
4. Graphologists do not study small letters.
5. When someone's handwriting has a backward slant, he or she probably also leaves letters open at the top.
6. Most shy people make big capital letters.
7. Most practical people make the lower part of a _g_ and a _j_ very large.

Words

See p. 45 for a list of other verbs taught in this unit.

I can't seem to . . .	copy (n, v)	typewriter	sale	kidnap	turn down
I'd better . . .	appointment	washing machine	kidnapper	be back	borrow
I'm supposed to . . .	report (n)	dry cleaning	dog	give back	expect
favor	instruction	repairman	chocolate cake	step out	by
line	photocopier	suit (n)	dial (v)	figure out	quietly

7. You're in great

People are exercising more than ever before. A recent Gallup poll shows that almost 50 percent of the adult population exercises daily. Why?

- Because when you're in good physical shape, you look and feel better.
- Because vigorous exercise helps prevent heart attacks and helps with weight control. It has also helped people with many different medical conditions, including diabetes, ulcers, nervous tension, high blood pressure, depression, and headaches.

1. **Read the paragraph about exercise. Then choose a partner and discuss these questions.**

1. How often do you exercise? What kinds of exercise do you like?
2. What kinds of exercise are popular in your country?

2. **You would like to get some exercise this Sunday. Choose a sport that you like. Then invite at least two other students to join you.**

Karen and Dennis run into a friend by the Charles River in Cambridge, Massachusetts. 🔲

A
- Mike
○ Dennis
▲ Karen

- Hi, Dennis! Hi, Karen!
○ Mike Bravo! Hey, you've lost a lot of weight, haven't you?
- Forty pounds.
○ No kidding! How much do you weigh now?
- Around 160.
▲ You're in great shape, Mike.
- Well, I get a lot of exercise.
○ I really ought to start doing something. I'm starting to get a potbelly.

shape!

B

● Do you ever get any exercise, Dennis?
○ Not regularly. I've always hated jogging.
● Well, why don't you do something else?
○ I enjoy biking. In fact, I used to go on long bike trips, but lately I can never seem to find the time.
● Well, here's your big chance. I'm biking to Lake Patunket next weekend with some friends of mine. How about joining us, both of you?
▲ Sounds great!
○ Well, I was planning to work Saturday. . . .
▲ Oh, come on, Dennis. You can work some other time. Uh, do you know where I can rent a bike, Mike?
● There's a bicycle shop somewhere around here. How tall are you?
▲ Five four.
● You're about the same height as my sister . . . or maybe an inch taller. She has two bikes. I'm sure you can borrow one of hers.

Figure it out

1. Say *Right, Wrong,* or *I don't know.*

1. Mike used to weigh 200 pounds.   *Right.*
2. Dennis used to exercise more.
3. Dennis likes to run.
4. Dennis has been too busy to take long bike trips.
5. Karen doesn't have her own bike.
6. Mike's sister is going to Lake Patunket next weekend, too.
7. Mike's sister is a year older than he is.
8. Mike and his sister don't like each other.

2. Fill in the blanks with *to work* or *working.*

1. I enjoy _working_ .
2. I was planning _____ .
3. I'm _____ tomorrow.
4. I used _____ harder.
5. How about _____ late?

C

○ Hey, I didn't know you had a sister, Mike.
● I have a twin sister.
○ Really! Is she just like you?
● Well, people say we look alike, but in most ways she's very different from me. Come to think of it, I guess we don't really have too much in common, but we get along really well.
○ Did you use to get along when you were younger?
● Yes. We've always gotten along well.
○ You're lucky. My brother and I used to fight all the time.

Ways to say it

1 TALK ABOUT WEIGHT

- You look great, *Mike.* You've *lost* (a lot of) weight, haven't you?
- ○ *Forty* pounds.
- No kidding! How much do you weigh now?
- ○ (I weigh) *160* (pounds).

Mike lost 40 pounds.	He used to weigh 200.
Lucy lost 35 pounds.	She used to weigh 140.
Dave gained 20 pounds.	He used to weigh 130.
Joan gained 15 pounds.	She used to weigh 90.

> 1 pound (lb) = 0.45 kilogram (kg)
> 1 kilogram = 2.2 pounds

▶

Pounds	Kilograms	Kilograms	Pounds
5	2.3	2	4.4
10	4.5	5	11
25	11.4	10	22
50	22.7	25	55
100	45.5	50	110

For more weights and measures, see p. 135.

2 TALK ABOUT HEIGHT

- How tall are you?
- ○ *Five four.*

> five four = five feet four inches (5'4")

- Oh, you're *an inch* [shorter / taller] than I am.
- You're the same height as I am.

> 1 meter (m) = 3.28 feet
> 1 foot (ft) = 0.30 meter
> 1 inch (in) = 2.54 centimeters

Feet and inches:	5'	5'2"	5'4"	5'6"	5'8"	5'10"	6'
Meters:	1.52	1.57	1.63	1.68	1.73	1.78	1.83

3 TALK ABOUT EXERCISE

- Do you ever get any exercise?
- ○ *I run five miles a day.* How about you?
- *Hardly ever. I ought to exercise more, but I can never seem to find the time.*

> five miles (mi) a day = five miles every day

Do you ever get any exercise?
I run five miles a day.
I play tennis every other day.
I roller-skate from time to time.
I go biking (bicycling) once in a while.
I used to swim, but I haven't lately.
Hardly ever. I ought to exercise more, but I can never seem to find the time.

> ought to = should

4  INFINITIVES VS. GERUNDS

I love I like I hate I've started	to swim. swimming.
I enjoy I've stopped	swimming.

> Gerunds, such as *swimming*, are formed the same way as present participles.

52

5 TALK ABOUT LIKES AND DISLIKES

● Do you like to *swim?*

○ Yes, I've always | liked / enjoyed | *swimming.*   ○ No, I've | never liked / always hated | *swimming.*

(In fact, I've started *swimming* regularly.)

Do you like to . . . ?	
swim	roller-skate
jog	ice-skate
play tennis	ski

6 Close-up

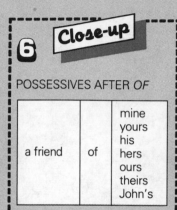

POSSESSIVES AFTER *OF*

		mine
		yours
		his
a friend	of	hers
		ours
		theirs
		John's

7 INVITE SOMEONE

● I'm going *biking* with *Bill and a friend* of *ours on Saturday.* How about joining us?

○ Sounds great.   ○ Well, I was planning to *work on Saturday.*

Ways you've said it
Would you like to join us? (formal)
Do you want to come along? (informal)

Some activities
Go biking with Bill and a mutual friend.
Go skiing with one of your friends.
Go canoeing with Nancy and one of her cousins.
Go hiking with one of your sister's friends.
Go camping with Ted and some of his friends.

8 ASK WHERE TO GET SOMETHING

● Do you know where I can *rent a bike?*

○ There's a *bicycle shop* on *Main Street.* It's called "*Wheels.*"   ○ Oh, I have *one* (I never use). You can borrow mine.

You'd like to . . .	You should go to a . . .
rent a bike.	sporting-goods store.
get your bike fixed.	bicycle shop.
buy a backpack.	ski shop.
buy a sleeping bag.	
rent skis.	
buy a tennis racket.	

9 TALK ABOUT YOUR FAMILY

● Is your *sister* older than you or younger?

○ *She's five years older.*   ○ We're | the same age.
                                          | twins.

● Do you have a lot in common?

○ Yes. We're a lot alike. *She's* interested in *photography,* too, and we both enjoy *doing things outdoors.*

○ Not really. Our interests are very different. *She likes . . .*

Identical twins

Fraternal twins

10

● Is your *sister* like you?

○ Actually, | *she's* a lot like me. | ○ *She's* totally different from me.
            | we're very similar. | We're completely different.

                                       She's a lot *quieter.*

● Do you get along?
○ *Yes. Most of the time.*
● Did you use to get along when you were younger?

○ Yes. We've always gotten along well.   ○ Not too well. We used to fight a lot.

get   got   gotten

11 Close-up

THE PAST WITH *USED TO*

Where	did you	use to	work?	
	Did you		drive	to work?

I	used to	take the bus to work.
	didn't use to	drive to work, but I do now.

Use *used to* to refer to something that took place repeatedly or over an extended period of time:

I used to take the bus to work.
I used to live in Washington.

12

Amy Sanchez started a new job a few months ago. Complete her conversation with Jim Stone, another employee. Use a form of *used to* and the verb in parentheses in each answer.

Jim: *What did you use to do* before you came here? (do)

Amy: I was marketing director at Lowell and White.

Jim: Oh, then you _____ with Don Ford. (work)

Amy: Yes, as a matter of fact, we're very good friends.

Jim: _____ a lot for that job, too? (travel)

Amy: Hardly ever. That's something I love about this job. Of course I work harder now. I _____ late at the office on my old job, (stay) and I _____ on weekends, either. (work)

A little exercise will do you good.

Doug is moving out of his apartment.

1

Ricky: Hey, what did you put in this box? It weighs a ton.

Doug: Oh, stop complaining. A little exercise will do you good.

Ricky: I get plenty of exercise already. I play basketball every day. In fact, I was planning to play today.

Doug: Well, we're almost finished. I guess I have more stuff than I thought. How about working, say, fifteen minutes more? Then we can order out for pizza. I'll treat.

Ricky: Sounds great. I'm so hungry I could eat a horse.

Sarah: Where do you want me to put this, Doug?

Doug: Hey, isn't that too heavy for you, Sarah?

Sarah: This is nothing. I lift weights.

Doug: Well, here, let me help you anyway. (*Grunts*) This box is heavier than I thought.

Ricky: I guess a little exercise would do *you* good. Maybe you ought to lift weights like Sarah.

Doug: Maybe I should. I used to be a lot stronger.

Sarah: You mean when you were young?

Doug: Funny, I thought I still was.

2. Figure it out

Say *Right*, *Wrong*, or *I don't know*.

1. Ricky hardly ever gets any exercise.   *Wrong.*
2. Doug, Ricky, and Sarah started working more than an hour ago.
3. Doug, Ricky, and Sarah are going to order pizza in fifteen minutes.
4. Doug is going to pay for the pizza.
5. Doug isn't as strong as he was when he was younger.

3. Listen in

Sarah and Doug continue their conversation. Read the questions below. Then listen to the conversation and answer them.

1. How tall is Ruth?
2. What has Ruth always enjoyed doing?

Your turn

Fill out this questionnaire for your partner. Ask your partner questions to get all the information you need. Then fill out the test for yourself. If you receive a low score, remember that it's never too late to change. What changes do you think you should make in your life?

Say it right

Say the phrases below. Then practice the conversation.

a friend of Pat's
     [s]

some friends of Bill's
       [z]

a cousin of Lois's
     [əz]

● I'm going skiing with Pat and some friends of Bill's on Saturday. One of them is a cousin of Lois's.
○ Really? A friend of Pat's called me last night and invited me, too. But I don't ski.

How Long Will You Live?

None of us know how long we will live, but we do know that certain factors can lengthen or shorten a person's life. Use the questionnaire below to calculate (approximately) how many years you will live.

START WITH THE NUMBER 72.   _72_

1. SEX
If you are a man,	subtract 3 ____
If you are a woman,	add 4 ____

2. LIFESTYLE
If you live in a big city (over 2 million),	−3 ____
If you live in a small town (under 10,000),	+2 ____
If you work at a desk,	−3 ____
If your work requires physical activity,	+3 ____
If you exercise a lot (5 times a week for 30 minutes),	+2 ____
If you live with someone,	+5 ____
If you live alone,	−1 ____

3. PERSONALITY
If you sleep more than 10 hours a night,	−4 ____
If you sleep less than 5 hours a night,	−4 ____
If you are impatient,	−3 ____
If you are easygoing,	+3 ____
If you are happy,	+1 ____
If you are unhappy,	−2 ____

4. SUCCESS
If you earn over $50,000 a year,	−2 ____
If you finished college,	+1 ____
If you have more than one college degree,	+2 ____
If you are 65 years old and still working,	+3 ____

5. FAMILY BACKGROUND
If any of your grandparents lived to 85,	+2 ____
If all four of your grandparents lived to 80,	+6 ____
If either of your parents died of a heart attack before 50,	−4 ____
If any parent, brother, or sister has heart disease or diabetes,	−3 ____

6. HEALTH
If you smoke more than 2 packs of cigarettes a day,	−8 ____
If you smoke more than half a pack of cigarettes a day,	−3 ____
If you are overweight by	
50 pounds,	−8 ____
30 pounds,	−3 ____
15 pounds,	−2 ____
If you have a medical exam every year,	+2 ____

7. AGE ADJUSTMENT
If you are 30−40,	+2 ____
40−50,	+3 ____
50−70,	+4 ____
If you are over 70,	+5 ____

YOU WILL LIVE APPROXIMATELY ____ YEARS.

On your own

An exercise program for the traveler.

SAS takes care of you . . .

The human body is made to move and it works best when it gets regular exercise. These days, however, we spend a lot of time sitting down — in an office chair, at the theater, or in a comfortable airline seat — where there is very little freedom of movement. To help solve this problem, SAS offers you this simple exercise program which will help keep you feeling good on long trips so that you arrive fresh and relaxed.

1. Jogging on the spot.
A warm-up exercise.
Lift your heels as high as possible, one foot at a time. At the same time, lift your arms in a bent position and move forward and backward as if you were walking. Continue for 1–3 minutes.

3. Forward bending with stomach in.
For your stomach muscles.
Pull in your stomach. Bend forward while lifting your toes high. Put your toes back on the floor, relax your stomach, and sit up again. Repeat 30 times.

5. Hand turning.
For your wrists.
Turn your hands over and open your fingers. Return your hands to their first position and relax them. Repeat 15 times.

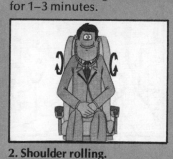

2. Shoulder rolling.
For shoulder joints and muscles.
Move your shoulders gently in large circles in both forward and backward directions. Repeat 6 times in each direction.

4. Head turning and nodding.
For your neck and spine.
Turn the head all the way to the right. Nod a few times. Do the same to the left. Repeat 6 times on each side.

6. Knees and elbows.
For blood circulation.
Raise your right knee to your left elbow. Then raise your left knee to your right elbow. Repeat 10 times.

---

1. Read the pamphlet from Scandinavian Airlines. Then match the parts of the body with the words below.

a. heel ⑧
b. elbow
c. neck
d. toes
e. fingers
f. stomach
g. shoulder
h. head
i. hand
j. foot
k. arm
l. knee

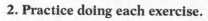

2. Practice doing each exercise.

1. Which exercise is the easiest for you?
2. Which exercise is the hardest for you?

Words

See p. 52 for a list of weights, measures, and frequency expressions, and pp. 52–53 for a list of sports.

get something fixed	sleeping bag	sporting-goods store	the same as	gain weight	hate (v)
It's called . . .	backpack	marketing director	different from	weigh	stop (v)
a lot in common	tennis racket	interest (n)	alike	ought to	fight (v)
No kidding!	bicycle shop	twin	outdoors	plan to	get along
	ski shop	height	regularly	rent (v)	gotten (get)

8. Review

Reception

Meg Wilson of Philadelphia and Jim Harris of Baltimore have just gotten married. Now the guests are enjoying themselves at the reception.

Brian: Nice party, isn't it?
Debbie: Yes, it really is. I'm afraid I don't know many people, though.
Brian: Oh, well, I'm Brian Cooper. I'm a friend of Meg's.
Debbie: Hi, Brian. My name's Debbie Burns.
Brian: How do you know Meg and Jim?
Debbie: Jim and I are cousins.
Brian: Oh, then you must be from Baltimore.
Debbie: No, I'm from the New York branch of the family. My parents are from Baltimore originally, but they moved to New York before I was born. Are you British?
Brian: You mean you can still tell after all these years in the States? Everyone in England thinks I have an American accent.
Debbie: Well . . . let's just say it's different from mine. How long have you been here?
Brian: Six years—the first two in Boston, the last four in Philly.
Debbie: This is my first trip to Philadelphia.
Brian: How do you like it?
Debbie: Well, I haven't seen anything yet. I just got in yesterday, and I haven't had a minute free.
Brian: What do you do in New York?
Debbie: I repair bicycles.
Brian: Do you? Do you work in a shop?
Debbie: Yes. Actually, I have my own shop.
Brian: The shop is yours, is it? That's interesting. Oh, look, there's a good friend of mine over there. Come on, I'll introduce you to him.

These statements are wrong. Correct them.

1. Debbie's parents still live in Baltimore.
   They don't live in Baltimore anymore. They live in New York.
2. Brian has lived in Philadelphia since he was a child.
3. Debbie has been to Philadelphia once before.
4. All of Jim's relatives live in Baltimore.
5. Debbie has lived in New York most of her life.
6. Debbie doesn't like Philadelphia.
7. Brian lives in Boston now.
8. Debbie works at a friend's bicycle shop.
9. Brian doesn't have a British accent anymore.
10. Brian wants to introduce Debbie to a friend of Jim's.

2 Act out the conversation, playing the role of Brian, Ken, or Debbie. Use the information below and the information in the dialogue.

Brian

Introduce Jim's cousin Debbie to your friend Ken Hunter. You'll need this information:
- You're a carpenter and so is Ken. You've known Ken for three years. You used to work together.
- Meg and Ken are old friends from high school.

Ken

Your friend Brian introduces you to Jim's cousin Debbie. You'll need this information:
- You've known Brian for three years. You're both carpenters, and you used to work together.
- You and Meg went to high school together.

Debbie

Brian introduces you to his friend Ken. Find out how long they've known each other and what they do.

Brian: Debbie, I'd like you to meet my friend Ken. . . .

3 Continue the conversation you started in exercise 2. Play the role of Ken or Debbie.

Ken

Find out where Debbie lives, and if she's ever been to Philadelphia. If she hasn't, invite her to go sightseeing tomorrow. You're taking some of Meg's friends.

Debbie

Answer Ken's questions. You've never been to Philadelphia, and you'll only be there for two more days. You'd like to go sightseeing, but you might be busy with relatives.

Ken: Where do you live, Debbie? . . .

4 Here are parts of some of the other conversations taking place at the reception. Say each one in a different way, using the words in parentheses.

1. ● Do you two know each other? (met)
   ○ No, I don't believe we've met.
   ● *Have you two met?*
   ○ *No, I don't believe we have.*

2. ● When did you meet Meg? (How long)
   ○ In 1980.

3. ● How long have you lived here? (always)
   ○ Since I was five. Before that I lived in Ohio.

4. ● Have you always lived in Philadelphia? (a long time)
   ○ No, I've only lived here for about a month. (moved)

5. ● When did you meet Meg? (just)
   ○ Years ago. We're very old friends. (mine)

6. ● Have you known Jim long? (When)
   ○ I've known him for about six years. (met) We went to the University of Maryland together. (both)

5 Meg is dancing with her uncle. Read the statements below. Then listen to the conversation and say *Right* or *Wrong*.

1. Meg works for an eye doctor.
2. Meg's uncle hasn't met Jim yet.
3. Meg and Jim went to the same university.

Excuse me, please . . .

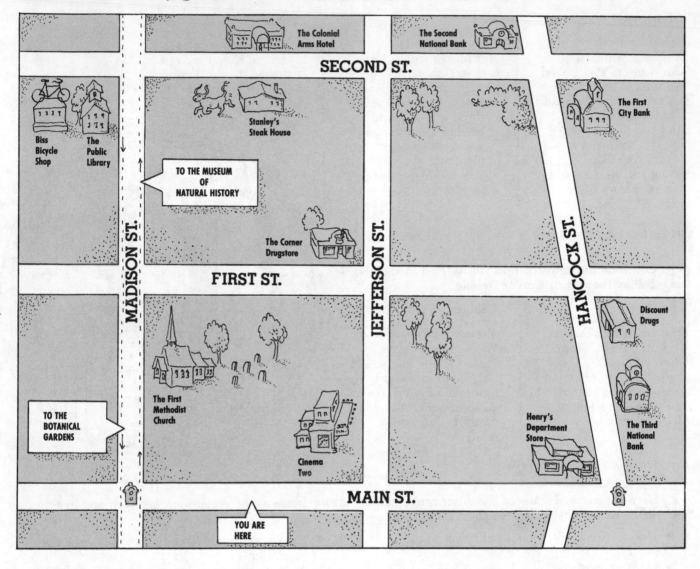

Using the map, figure out a question for each conversation. Then combine each pair of sentences in brackets. [ ]

1. ● *Do you know of any hotels around here* ?
   ○ There's one about three blocks from here. [Walk to the corner. Then turn left on Jefferson.] [Stay on Jefferson. You'll get to Second Street.] Turn left. It'll be on your right, about halfway down the block.

   When you get to the corner, turn left on Jefferson. Stay on Jefferson until you get to Second Street.

2. ● _____ ?
   ○ Take the Madison Street bus. It goes right there. [Walk to the corner. Then turn right.] That's Madison Street. [Then go straight ahead. You'll come to a big church.] The bus stop's right in front of it.

3. ● _____ ?
   ○ Yes, it's the next street after Jefferson. [Just stay on Main. You'll come to a traffic light.] There'll be a big department store on your left. You can't miss it.

4. ● _____ ?
   ○ Go straight ahead. [You'll pass a big department store. Just after it, turn left.] It'll be on your right about halfway down the block.

2 Read these conversations and, using the map on p. 60, figure out what the people are talking about in each one. Then complete each conversation with an appropriate expression.

1. ● Is it nice?
   ○ Well, I've never stayed there, but _I've heard it is_ .

   They're talking about The Colonial Arms Hotel.

2. ● Is it good?
   ○ Yes. _____ , and everything was delicious.

3. ● Is it interesting?
   ○ _____ there, but it's supposed to have some good exhibits.

4. ● Is it crowded at lunchtime?
   ○ I don't know. _____ . I always go there in the morning, as soon as I get my check.

5. ● Do they do good work?
   ○ Well, I don't have a bicycle, but _____ .

3 Fill in the blanks with the superlative forms of the adjectives in parentheses.

1. There are three banks near here. _The closest_ one is on Hancock near Main. (close)

2. There's a good movie theater on the next block. In fact, I think it shows _____ movies in town. (good)

3. _____ hotel in town is on Second Street, but it's also _____ . (modern, expensive)

4. The restaurant across from the Colonial Arms Hotel on Second Street has _____ service and is one of _____ ones around. (fast, reasonable) It's also one of _____ . (old)

5. Henry's is _____ department store in town. (big)

6. You should go see the new library. It's _____ building in town. (unusual)

4 A young woman has just left the library on Second Street and is looking for a shoe-repair shop. Read the statements below. Then listen to the conversation and say *Right* or *Wrong*.

1. Ed's Shoe Repair is closer than Tony's.
2. Ed's is fifteen minutes away by taxi.

5 You're riding your bike and you get a flat tire right in front of Henry's Department Store. You stop someone on the street to get information. Act out the conversation.

● *Excuse me—do you know where . . . ?*

Have you seen any good movies lately?

Len Gold is talking to a friend of his, Lou Crosby. Complete the conversation using the words in parentheses. Pay careful attention to the tense of the verb.

Len: _Have you seen_ any good movies lately? (you/see)

Lou: No, but _____ a play last night—*Master Harold and the Boys.* (I/just/see)

Len: Oh, _____ it, (I/see) but _____ it's very good. (I/hear) How _____ it? (you/like)

Lou: _____ excellent. (it/be) Athol Fugard _____ it, you know. (write)*

Len: Oh! _____ a couple of his plays, (I/read) and _____ to see one of them. (I/always/want) Where _____ ? (it/play)

Lou: At the Wilbur.

Len: Oh, then _____ this weekend. (maybe/I/go) I think _____ Marilyn Wen. (I/invite)

Lou: _____ it. (she/already/see) _____ her at the theater last night. (I/see)

(* write   wrote   written)

62

2 Len calls two friends to invite them to go to the play. Listen to both conversations and end each one appropriately.

 3 Marilyn Wen talked to some friends about their plans for the weekend. What did each of them say? Use the expressions in the box and the information below.

> I might (not) . . .   I'm going to . . .
> I'm thinking of . . .   I'm supposed to . . .
> I was planning to . . .

1. Susan Garcia is working on Sunday, but maybe she'll go to the beach on Saturday.

   I'm going to work on Sunday, but . . .

2. John Weiner's parents expect him for dinner on Saturday, and his sister invited him over on Sunday. He's not feeling well, so maybe he'll stay home.

3. David Porras isn't sure what he's doing, but he has an idea: rent a car and drive to the mountains on either Saturday or Sunday.

4. Shelley Lipson's sister is leaving for Europe on Sunday, and Shelley has offered to take her to the airport. Shelley isn't busy on Saturday.

5. Carl Sato would like to go camping, but he hasn't made plans yet.

6. Ginny Gomes had plans to go camping, but now she's not sure if she's going. It's supposed to rain this weekend.

4 One of your friends calls and invites you to go see *Master Harold and the Boys* on Friday night. Choose one of the roles below and act out the conversation.

Role A

You haven't heard of the play. At first you're not sure you can go because you have an exam on Monday, but you want to do something interesting this weekend.

Role B

You've heard that the play is good, but you're not sure you'll be free Friday night. Give a reason why you might be busy.

Role C

You saw the play when it first opened. Suggest doing something else.

Happy Birthday, dear Martha!

Martha White, Sweetwater's oldest citizen, just celebrated her one hundredth birthday. A reporter was at the party and asked Mrs. White to talk about her life. 🔲

Martha White: Sweetwater's Oldest Citizen

Mrs. White, you've had a very long and a very full life.

Yes, I've been very fortunate.

Have you always lived in Sweetwater?

All my life. As a matter of fact, I was born in this house. Of course, I've taken many trips in my life. I've been all over the world. But I've always come back to Sweetwater. That's the way it used to be in the old days. You were born in a town, and you lived there until you died.

How many children did you have?

Six. First I had four boys and then two girls. The oldest is seventy-five now, and my baby is sixty-eight. And, of course, they all had children of their own, and their children had children. The last time I counted I had thirty great-grandchildren. So you see I've never felt lonely and I've never been bored. Who has time?

Your first husband died ten years ago . . .

Yes, at the age of ninety-two. We had seventy-three wonderful years together. We were very much alike, you know. Our greatest loves were music and the outdoors. And talking, too. Both of us loved a good conversation. People don't talk to each other anymore. They watch television.

Mrs. White, you've already lived a hundred years and you look as if you might live another hundred years. What's your secret?

Well, I've laughed a lot. That's very important. And I've kept busy. I taught school for over forty years. I've gotten a lot of exercise, too. I've always enjoyed sports—skiing, horseback riding, swimming. In fact, I still swim every day at the high school pool and now I've started jogging a little with my second husband.

When did you remarry?

Six years ago. I was ninety-four and he was a young man of eighty. A lot of people say I robbed the cradle!

You've done so much in your life. Is there anything you haven't done yet that you'd like to do someday?

Well, you know, I've read many, many books in my life, but I've never written one myself. So I'm writing one now. I'd like to finish it and maybe publish it. And now that I've started jogging, I think I'd like to run in a race—maybe even the Boston Marathon. Who knows?

Mrs. White, you're a hundred years old today. How do you feel?

Wonderful! Not a day over ninety!

🔲 Read about Martha White. Then change the tense of the verb in each of these statements so that they are true.

1. Mrs. White used to swim every day. *She still swims every day.*
2. Mrs. White wrote a book.
3. Mrs. White teaches school.
4. Mrs. White lived a hundred years.
5. Mrs. White has been married for seventy-three years.
6. Mrs. White has run in a race.

2 Read about Martha White's children and grandchildren. Then fill in the blanks, choosing from these expressions: *both of, a few of, all of, most of, one of, the other one,* or *the others.*

Martha White has six children. Her two daughters live in Sweetwater, Texas. Her older daughter lives next door and her younger daughter lives five minutes away. Her oldest son lives in Sweetwater, too, but she has three sons who live in Fort Worth, Texas. Seventeen of her twenty-one grandchildren live in Texas.

1. _____ Martha White's children live in Texas.
2. _____ her four sons still lives in Sweetwater.
   _____ live in Fort Worth.
3. _____ her daughters live in Sweetwater.
   _____ them lives next door, and _____ lives five minutes away.
4. _____ Martha White's grandchildren live in Texas, too.

 3 How have things changed since you or your parents were children? Make statements with *used to, didn't use to,* and *not . . . anymore.*

Here are some ways Martha White would answer this question: *People used to stay in the same town their whole lives. Now they move more. People don't talk to each other anymore. Now they watch television. . . .*

 4 Compare yourself to your mother or father. Are you alike or different? Try to be as specific as you can.

5 Pretend you're celebrating your one hundredth birthday. Write a short article about yourself, telling about things you've done in your life and things you'd still like to do. Before starting to write, follow the steps below:

1. Make a list of things you've done in your life (or places you've been).
2. Make a list of things you haven't done yet, but that you'd like to do someday.
3. Make a list of things you enjoy doing.

9. Let me just check

Dear Nancy,   June 10, 1984

So much has happened since the last time we saw each other. The big news is that I just got married to Lou Riley. He's a geologist. I met him here in Texas. I've been here for two years now, doing graduate work in archeology. I'd really like you to meet Lou. We'll be in Washington the week of July 2, and we'll be staying with my parents. I hope we can get together then. I'll give you a call when I get to town. Give my best to Dan, although he probably doesn't remember me. We only met that one time at Mary Ketchum's party.

See you soon!

Eileen

Try this

Act out the conversation, playing the role of Nancy Brown or her husband, Dan.

Nancy

You just received this letter from Eileen Riley, an old friend from college. Tell your husband, Dan, who Eileen is and what her plans are.

Dan

Your wife, Nancy, tells you about a letter she received from Eileen Riley. Act interested and ask a lot of questions. Find out who Eileen is and what she said.

Start like this:
Nancy: I just got a letter from Eileen Riley.
  Dan: Who's Eileen Riley? . . .

Nancy gets a phone call from Eileen Riley.

(A) ● Nancy Brown
     ○ Eileen Riley

● Hello?
○ Hello, Nancy? This is Eileen Riley.
● Eileen! How are you? Congratulations!
○ Thanks. I'm sorry to call so late. I hope I didn't wake you up.
● Oh, no. I haven't gone to bed yet. I was just watching TV.
○ Listen, are you and Dan doing anything on Saturday?
● I don't think we are.
○ Then how about coming over for dinner?
● I'd love to, but let me just check with Dan before I tell you for sure. He wasn't feeling well, so he went to bed early.
○ I hope it's nothing serious.

● No, I don't think it's anything to worry about. Just a cold. What time do you want us to come?
○ Oh, about seven. You've been to my parents' house, haven't you?
● Yes, but it's been a while. What's their address again?
○ It's 3820 Warren Street. It's off Wisconsin Avenue.
● Oh, yes, I think I remember now. Well, let's say tentatively that we're coming, and I'll let you know if we can't make it.
○ I really hope you can come.
● I do too. I can't wait to see you again. I haven't seen you for so long.
○ So . . . tell me what's happening in *your* life. . . .

with Dan.

● I got a call from Eileen Riley last night.
○ Who's that?
● Don't you remember? She's the one who just got married.
○ Oh, right, the archeologist. What does her husband do again?
● He's a geologist. Anyway, they'd like us to go to her parents' house for dinner Saturday.
○ We have theater tickets for Saturday, don't we?
● Oh, I completely forgot! I'd better call her back right now.

Figure it out

1. Say *Right*, *Wrong*, or *I don't know*.

1. Nancy didn't think she and Dan were busy Saturday.   *Right.*
2. Nancy wanted to ask Dan before she accepted Eileen's invitation.

3. Nancy was sleeping when Eileen called.
4. Dan gets colds often.
5. Nancy goes to Eileen's parents' house often.

2. Choose *a* or *b*.

1. I hope it's _____ .
   a. nothing serious
   b. anything serious

2. I don't think we're doing _____ .
   a. something
   b. anything

3. You've been there, _____ ?
   a. haven't you
   b. don't you

4. What time do you want _____ ?
   a. us to come
   b. we come

67

Ways to say it

1

┃ ╭─────────────────────────╮
┃ │ APOLOGIZE FOR   │
┃ │ CALLING AT A BAD TIME   │
┃ ╰─────────────────────────╯

- Hello?
- ○ Hello, *Nancy?* This is *Eileen.* I'm sorry to call *so late.*
- Oh, that's O.K. *I haven't gone to bed yet.*

I'm sorry to call . . .	Oh, that's O.K. . . .
so late.	I'm still up.
so early.	I haven't gone to bed yet.
at dinner time.	I've already finished eating.
	I've been up since six.
	I haven't started eating yet.
	I've been awake for hours.

2

- Hello?
- ○ Hello, *Nancy?* This is *Eileen.* I hope *I didn't wake you up.*
- Oh, no. I was just *watching TV.*

Some questions
Did I wake you up?
Did I get you out of bed?
Am I calling at a bad time?
Am I interrupting your dinner?

What you were doing when the phone rang	
watching TV	getting ready for work
making breakfast	listening to the radio
reading the paper	setting the table
doing the dishes	putting away the dishes

3

╭─────────────────────────╮
│ ASK IF SOMEONE HAS   │
│ PLANS   │
╰─────────────────────────╯

- Are you doing anything on *Saturday?*

○ I don't think | I am. / I'm busy. | ○ I think | I am. / I'm busy. |

○ But let me check my calendar. . . .

○ No, I'm not doing anything on *Saturday.*   ○ I'm sorry. I already have plans for *Saturday.*

╭────────────────────────────────────╮
│ Asking if someone has plans is a   │
│ very informal way of inviting   │
│ someone. In more formal situations,│
│ invite someone without asking if he│
│ or she has plans.   │
╰────────────────────────────────────╯

4 — INVITE SOMEONE TO YOUR HOUSE

● I haven't seen you (and *Dan*) for so long. How about coming over (for *dinner*) on *Saturday*?

○ *We*'d love to. What time do you want *us* to come?
● Oh, about *seven*.

○ I don't think *we're* doing anything, but let me just check (with *Dan*) and call you back.
● Sure. I hope you can make it.

Ways you've said it

Would you like to come over? (neutral)
Do you want to come over? (informal)
How about coming over? (informal)

---

5 — Close-up

HOPE AND THINK

Affirmative statements

| I | hope
think | (that) | I can make it.
I'll be on time. |

Negative statements

| I | hope | (that) | I'm **not** busy.
she **doesn't** have plans.
it's **nothing** serious. |

| I | **don't** think | (that) | I'm busy.
she has plans.
it's **anything** serious. |

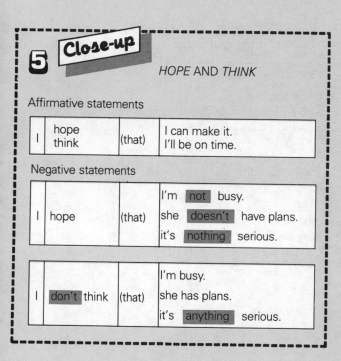

6

Rephrase the sentences in the letter using *hope* or *think*, as indicated.

I hope everything is O.K. with you. . . .

Dear Mary Lynn,

    Is everything O.K. with you? (hope) John has a cold, but it's nothing serious. (think) Does Paul like his new job? (hope) He won't be sorry he took it. (think)

    We can't come to Davenport this weekend, (think) but we can come next weekend. (think) Have you made plans yet? (hope)

    I didn't give you our new telephone number. (think) It's 234-5879. I'll see you soon. (hope)

               Love,

               Doris

---

7 — CHECK PLANS WITH SOMEONE

● *Eileen Riley* called last night. *She* | 'd like / invited / asked | us to come over *Saturday*.

○ But *we have theater tickets for Saturday, don't we?*
● Oh, I completely forgot! I'd better call *her* back right now.

Tag questions, such as *Don't we?*, are often used to confirm or clarify information.

But . . .

we have theater tickets for Saturday,	doesn't she?
we're going to a concert,	didn't she?
Diana wants us to come over,	don't we?
Carol invited us to go to the movies with her,	aren't we?

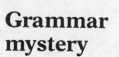

Grammar mystery

Mary can come, _____ she?
Joe will be there, _____ he?
We've already made plans, _____ we?

Close-up

INFINITIVES WITH SUBJECTS

She	'd like invited asked wants	me you him her us them	to come over. to go to the movies.

When the subject of an
infinitive is a pronoun,
it is an object pronoun.

---

9 **Complete the conversations as in the example, using the verbs in parentheses. There may be several possible answers.**

1. ● Who were you just talking to?
   ○ That was Jane. I _asked her to come over_ later. (come over)

2. ● Hi, Lynn. Did anyone call?
   ○ Harry did. He _____ dinner at his house. (have)

3. ● Are you busy tomorrow morning?
   ○ I think I am. Jane _____ shopping with her. (go)

4. ● Hi, Bill. How was your day?
   ○ Fine. I ran into Jane and Ted on my way home. I _____ tennis with us tomorrow. (play)

5. ● I'm back. Any messages?
   ○ Yes. Neil called right after you left. He _____ him with his French homework. (help)

---

10 **REFRESH YOUR MEMORY**

● *What's your address* again?
○ *It's 3820 Warren Street.*

Some things you've forgotten	
an address	a birthday
a phone number	where someone's from
a last name	what someone does

---

11 **IDENTIFY SOMEONE**

● I *got a phone call from Eileen Riley.*
○ Who's that?
● Don't you remember? *She's the one who just got married.*

You got a phone call from
Eileen Riley. She just got
married.

You ran into Ed Paxton the
other day. He was in your math
class.

You saw Pat Ripley in the
grocery store yesterday.
Pat just moved here from
England.

You got a letter from Mike Holt.
He's living in Sweden.

I was just passing through.

Kate Simmons stops by to see Doug at the recreation center.

1

Kate: Hi, Doug! I see you got the job. Congratulations!

Doug: Kate! What brings you to these parts?

Kate: I was just passing through. One of my elderly clients lives around here. So, how's it going?

Doug: Well, so far, so good. Things are still a little confusing, or should I say, I'm a little confused. . . .

Kate: Well, it's only your first week. Listen, tomorrow is Gloria's Smith's last day and we're having a little party for her at the agency. You've met Gloria, haven't you?

Doug: Let's see. . . . Gloria . . . is she the one who sits by the window?

Kate: That's right—the one with the long red hair. Anyway, Mr. Dow wanted me to tell you to be sure and come.

Doug: Oh, well, I'll definitely try to make it. What time should I be there?

Kate: Oh, about a quarter to five. So, are you all settled?

Doug: I wish I were. I'm still looking for an apartment. If you hear of anything . . .

Kate: Actually, a good friend of mine, Terry Enders, just moved into a newly renovated building. I can ask her if there are any apartments there.

Doug: Oh, thanks. That would be great. What did you say your friend's name was?

Kate: Terry . . . Terry Enders. Why, do you know her?

Doug: No, I don't think I do. But the name rings a bell.

2. Figure it out

Say *Right, Wrong,* or *I don't know.*

1. This is the first time Kate has seen Doug since he got the job.   *Right.*
2. Doug doesn't know who Gloria is.
3. Doug has already met everyone at the Community Services Agency.
4. There are some empty apartments in Terry Enders' building.
5. Doug has worked at his new job less than a week.
6. Doug is staying at a hotel.

3. Listen in

Kate calls Terry about an apartment for Doug. Read Kate's part of the conversation below. Then, as you listen to Terry, put the sentences in the right order.

___ Yes, that's right. He just moved to Chicago.

1 Hello, Terry? This is Kate.

___ O.K., let me just get a pencil. (*Returns with pencil*) O.K. . . .

___ What was the number again?

___ A friend of mine, Doug Lee, needs an apartment. Are there any in your building?

Your turn

Eating customs differ from country to country. Describe how each person is eating using the words under each picture. Then discuss these questions in groups:

1. Where do you think these people are from?
2. Are any of these customs similar to yours?
3. Which customs are different from yours?
4. What are some of the eating customs in your country?
5. What other interesting eating customs have you seen?

eat—hands

peel an orange—knife—fork

eat—chopsticks

right hand—left hand—lap

Say it right

Practice the tag questions below. Then practice the conversation.

That chicken looks good, doesn't it? (falling intonation)   You're hungry, aren't you? (rising intonation)

- ● That chicken looks good, doesn't it?
- ○ It really does.
- ● You're hungry, aren't you?
- ○ Yes, I am.
- ● Well, then let's have some.

Say tag questions with rising intonation when you are asking a true question and aren't sure the other person will agree with you. Say them with falling intonation when you are almost sure the other person will agree.

72

On your own

Read the advice column. Then say *Right* or *Wrong*.

1. You should never bring dessert to a dinner. *Wrong.*
2. You should arrive at a dinner five to ten minutes late.
3. One way to politely refuse food is to say, "I don't want any."
4. You should leave the napkin on the table when you eat.
5. The last utensils to use will be the closest to your plate.
6. In the United States most people eat with the fork in their left hand.
7. You should thank your host or hostess twice—when you leave and the next day.

Ask Diana Wilkins

If you've just arrived in the United States…
by Diana Wilkins

DEAR DIANA:
I have only lived in the United States for two months. I have met many people, and some of them have invited me to dinner at their homes. The trouble is that I always get so nervous on these occasions. I'm so afraid that I will do something that is inappropriate in the United States. Could you please tell me what some of the most important rules are?
—CONFUSED

DEAR CONFUSED:
Your reaction to dinner invitations is quite natural, and I have received many letters on this topic from people new to the United States. Therefore, I have made a list of some of the specific rules to follow:

- If the dinner is informal, ask if you can bring something, such as something to drink or dessert.
- Arrive five to ten minutes late, but never early. Your host or hostess may still be getting ready.
- Take off your hat and coat as soon as you enter someone's home.
- Feel free to politely refuse food that you don't want. Say, "No, thanks. I don't care for any."
- Put your napkin on your lap before you begin to eat.
- If there are a number of utensils, those farthest from the plate are supposed to be used first. The last utensils to be used will be on the inside.
- Hold the fork in your right hand unless you are left-handed.
- Keep your left hand in your lap unless you are cutting something.
- Remember to thank your host or hostess when you leave. You should also telephone the next day to say thank you again.

These are some of the basic guidelines, and, of course, they may vary with the situation. When in doubt, it is best to look at what the other people at the dinner table are doing.

Words

Let me (just) . . .	calendar	right hand	run into	awake
geologist	dinner time	left hand	wake someone up	up
archeology	meat	check (v)	put away	
graduate work	lap	peel (v)	make it	
	chopsticks	interrupt		

10. Tell us about

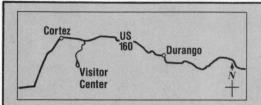

Mesa Verde National Park

(10 mi E of Cortez, 36 mi W of Durango, on US 160 to park entrance, then 16 mi S to Visitor Center) **Elevation** 7,000 ft (2,134 m) at park headquarters.

Mesa Verde, Spanish for "green table," is a large plateau which rises 1,500 to 2,000 feet (457 to 610 meters) above the valleys around it. It was the home of Native Americans for more than 800 years and it is famous for well-preserved cliff dwellings in its canyon walls.

The park is open all year. The public campgrounds, 4 miles (6 kilometers) from the park entrance, are open from May to October.

Cliff dwellings are houses in cliffs.

Try this

1. **Read the article. Then choose a partner and discuss these questions:**

   1. What places should tourists visit in your country?
   2. Why should they go there?

2. **Tell your partner about an interesting vacation that you've taken. Answer these questions:**

   1. Where did you go?
   2. Where did you stay?
   3. What did you do?
   4. Did you have a good time?

A
● Molly
△ Jack
○ Sue
▲ Ken

Molly and Jack Stone have just come back from a trip to the Southwest. They have invited Sue and Ken Molnar over for dinner. 📼

● Here are some cookies that I made. Help yourselves.
○ Oh, Molly, you've gone to so much trouble.
● It was no trouble at all.
△ Would anyone care for coffee or tea?
○ I'll have a cup of coffee, please.
▲ Make that two.
△ Molly?
● I don't care for anything, thanks.
○ So, don't keep us in suspense. Tell us about your trip.

● Well, I'd say it was the nicest vacation we've ever taken, wouldn't you, Jack?
△ Without a doubt. You really ought to go. You won't be disappointed.
● The scenery is spectacular.
△ And the cliff dwellings were fascinating.
● Jack and I are very interested in archeology.
△ Would you like to see our slides? We just got them back today.
▲ Hmm . . . it might be a little late for . . .
○ Oh, of course. We'd love to see them.

your trip.

B

- That's the camper that we rented.
- ○ Did you have all your meals in it?
- We usually ate at least one meal out every day.
- △ To tell you the truth, the restaurants were a little disappointing.

(Change of slide)

- Do you remember where this was, Jack?
- △ Yes, that's Mesa Verde National Park.
- ▲ Where exactly is that? Near Denver?
- △ No, it's in southwestern Colorado. Denver's about 250 miles northeast of it.
- ○ Who's the woman who's standing behind Jack?
- Oh, the one with the hat? She's just someone we met at the park.
- △ Hmm . . . I don't recognize her.
- Don't you remember? She's the one we had dinner with.
- △ Oh, yes. That's right.

(Change of slide)

- Oh, look! That's the mule I rode in the Grand Canyon.
- ○ That sounds exciting! . . .

Figure it out

1. Say *Right*, *Wrong*, or *I don't know*.

1. Molly bought the cookies in a store. *Wrong.*
2. Molly doesn't want anything to drink.
3. Molly and Jack spent two weeks in the Southwest.
4. Molly and Jack have their own camper.
5. Molly and Jack thought the restaurants were excellent.

2. Choose *a* or *b*.

1. Here's a cake _____ I made.
   a. who
   (b.) that

2. I'm very interested _____ history.
   a. in
   b. with

3. Do you remember where _____ ?
   a. it was
   b. was it

4. I was _____ in the restaurants.
   a. disappointed
   b. disappointing

5. The trip was _____ .
   a. fascinated
   b. fascinating

Ways to say it

1 OFFER FOOD AND DRINK

● Here *are some cookies (that I made).* Help yourselves.
○ Oh, thank you. (You've gone to so much trouble.)
● Would anyone care for *coffee or tea?*
○ I'll have *a cup of coffee,* please.   ○ I don't care for anything, thanks.
● *Ken? . . .*

Some food
some cookies
some sandwiches
a chocolate cake

Some drinks
a cup of coffee (tea)
a glass of lemonade (iced tea, water)
a can of soda

Ways you've said it
Would you care for . . . ?   (formal)
Would you like . . . ?   (neutral)
Do you want . . . ?   (informal)

2 TALK ABOUT A VACATION

● How was your trip to *Colorado?*
○ Great. *The scenery was spectacular. . . .*   ○ Not too good. *I was bored most of the time.*
● It sounds wonderful.   ● Oh, I'm sorry to hear that.

Some reasons why your trip was good	Some reasons why your trip was bad
The scenery was spectacular.	I was bored most of the time.
The weather was fantastic.	There was nothing interesting to do at night.
The museums were fascinating.	The restaurants were overpriced.
The food was excellent.	I was disappointed in the food.
The people were very friendly.	

3 TALK ABOUT YOUR COUNTRY

Someone who has never been to your country is planning a vacation. Try to convince him or her to take a trip there.

● You really ought to go to *Brazil.* You won't be disappointed.
○ Tell me something about it.
● *The countryside is magnificent, and the people are very friendly. . . .*

Harry is bored.

4 Close-up

PRESENT VS. PAST PARTICIPLES

Present participles	
The movie was	interesting. disappointing. boring. shocking.

Past participles			
I was	interested disappointed bored shocked	in in by by	the movie.

Harry is boring.

5 Read the weekly column in *Literary News*. Then fill in each blank with an appropriate participle and, where necessary, a preposition. Choose from the list below.

The historical parts were very interesting . . .

boring, bored (by)
depressing, depressed (by)
disappointing, disappointed (in)
exciting, excited (by)
fascinating, fascinated (by)
interesting, interested (in)
shocking, shocked (by)

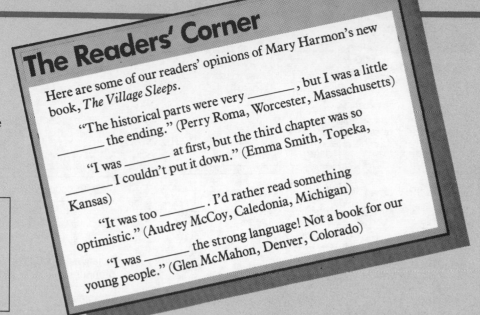

The Readers' Corner

Here are some of our readers' opinions of Mary Harmon's new book, *The Village Sleeps.*

"The historical parts were very _____, but I was a little _____ the ending." (Perry Roma, Worcester, Massachusetts)

"I was _____ at first, but the third chapter was so _____ I couldn't put it down." (Emma Smith, Topeka, Kansas)

"It was too _____. I'd rather read something optimistic." (Audrey McCoy, Caledonia, Michigan)

"I was _____ the strong language! Not a book for our young people." (Glen McMahon, Denver, Colorado)

---

6 (SAY WHERE YOU LIVE)

- Where do you live in *Italy?*
- In *Modena.*
- Where exactly is that?
- It's in the *northern* part of the country. It's about *25* miles *northwest* of *Bologna.*

Some locations		
in the	northern southern eastern western central	part
on the (Atlantic) coast		

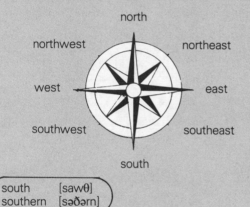

north
northwest   northeast
west   east
southwest   southeast
south

▶ | south | [sawθ] |
| southern | [səðərn] |

---

7 (IDENTIFY SOMEONE)

Identify the people in the picture. Here are some verbs you can use: *hold, stand, wear, laugh,* and *sit.*

- Who's the *woman* | with *the baby?*
who's *holding the baby?*

- Oh, *she's* someone | (who) (that) | *I went to school with.*

▲

When the relative pronoun is the *object* of a verb or preposition, it may be omitted:

He's someone + I know *him* from work
  ▶ He's someone I know from work.
She's someone + I went to school *with her*
  ▶ She's someone I went to school *with.*

How you know each person

1. I went to school with her.   4. I've known her for years.
2. I know him from work.   5. I used to work with him.
3. I grew up with her.

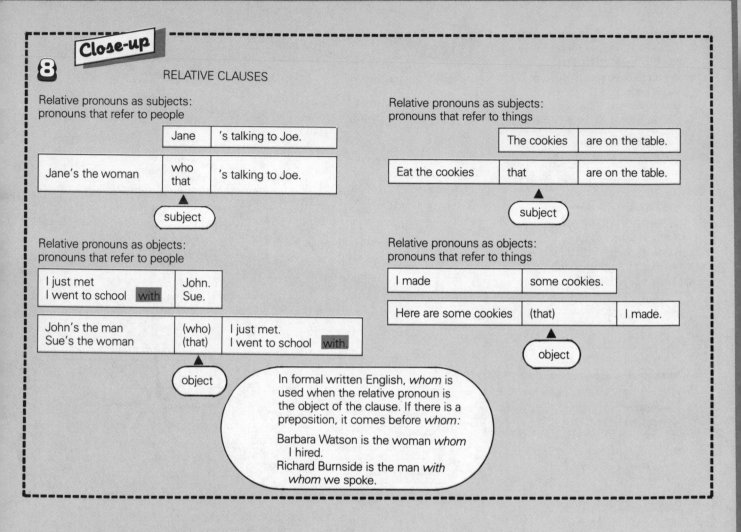

Close-up

8 RELATIVE CLAUSES

Relative pronouns as subjects:
pronouns that refer to people

Jane	's talking to Joe.

Jane's the woman	who that	's talking to Joe.

▲ subject

Relative pronouns as subjects:
pronouns that refer to things

	The cookies	are on the table.

Eat the cookies	that	are on the table.

▲ subject

Relative pronouns as objects:
pronouns that refer to people

I just met I went to school with	John. Sue.

John's the man Sue's the woman	(who) (that)	I just met. I went to school with.

▲ object

Relative pronouns as objects:
pronouns that refer to things

I made	some cookies.

Here are some cookies	(that)	I made.

▲ object

In formal written English, *whom* is used when the relative pronoun is the object of the clause. If there is a preposition, it comes before *whom:*

Barbara Watson is the woman *whom* I hired.
Richard Burnside is the man *with whom* we spoke.

9 Read the letter. Then combine each pair of sentences in brackets into one sentence with a relative clause.

Mesa Verde is a national park that's located in southwestern Colorado. . . .

Dear Nancy and Tom,   Saturday, May 15

I just got back from a wonderful trip to Mesa Verde. Have you been there? [Mesa Verde is a national park. The park is located in southwestern Colorado.] [I went there with some people. I work with them.] All of us were interested in Cliff Palace, the park's largest cliff dwelling. It has more than 217 rooms and 23 kivas. ["Kiva" is a Hopi word. The word means "ceremonial room."] [The guide was excellent. The guide showed us the cliff dwelling.] [He told us a lot of interesting things about the Native Americans. The Native Americans lived in the cliff dwelling.] It was fascinating. It was

78

He hasn't been himself.

Laura and Terry's parents are visiting them in Chicago, and they've all gone to the Museum of Science and Industry. 📼

1

Mr. Enders: This is one of the finest museums I've ever been to, and I've been to a lot of museums. It's a shame Chuck couldn't make it. We've seen so little of him this trip.

Laura: Well, he hasn't been himself lately.

Mr. Enders: Is he still upset about the job?

Laura: Yes, he was really disappointed.

Mr. Enders: Well, he can't go on being depressed forever. He has to start looking for something else.

Laura: Oh, he has. Actually, there *is* one possibility, but I'm not too excited about it.

Mr. Enders: Why not? It's not a good job?

Laura: Oh, no, it's a great job—very similar to the one he didn't get. It's an even larger recreation program, but it's in Portland, Oregon. Chuck has a brother who lives there.

Mr. Enders: Does it look promising?

Laura: No, I really don't think he'll get it, and, well, I know this sounds selfish, but in a way I'm relieved. I mean, Portland's two thousand miles from here.

2. Figure it out

Say *Right, Wrong,* or *I don't know.*

1. Laura's parents have met Chuck before.   *Right.*
2. Chuck has been too depressed to start looking for another job.
3. Laura hopes Chuck will get the job in Portland.
4. Chuck's brother told him about the job.
5. Laura doesn't want Chuck to move so far away.

3. Listen in 📼

Terry and Mrs. Enders join Laura and Mr. Enders. Read the statement below. Then listen to the conversation and choose *a* or *b*.

The Enderses are going to eat _____ .
a. at Laura's house
b. at a restaurant

Your turn

Moonlight Travel Agency sponsored a "Win a trip" contest, and you and your partner have just won a vacation for two. You can choose to go to any one of the four cities below. Discuss the attractions of each place, and decide with your partner where you will take your vacation.

Moonlight Travel Agency

WIN A TRIP FOR TWO!!

HONOLULU, Hawaii
Attractions:
- sun, sea, and sand
- great nightlife
- Polynesian food
- warm climate all year round

PARIS, France
Attractions:
- sightseeing
- shopping — clothes and perfume
- art museums
- delicious food
- romantic views

CAIRO, Egypt
Attractions:
- the Pyramids
- shopping — crafts, jewelry, and cotton clothing
- fascinating culture
- 3,000 years of history

RIO DE JANEIRO, Brazil
Attractions:
- nightlife — great music and dance
- shopping — jewelry and crafts
- Copacabana Beach
- beautiful rain forests

 **Say it right**

Say the words below. Then practice the conversation. ▭

interesting [íntrəstiŋ]   fascinating [fǽsineytiŋ]   exciting [iksáytiŋ]   disappointing [disəpɔ́yntiŋ]

- How was your trip?
- ○ Great. There were so many interesting things to see, and the museums were fascinating.
- It sounds exciting. How was the food?
- ○ Well, a little disappointing, but not too bad.

On your own

Read the encyclopedia articles. Then find each of the words below, and say whether it is used as a noun, a verb, or an adjective.

1. Egyptian *adjective*
2. Egypt
3. Egyptologist
4. king
5. kingdom
6. ruled
7. rule
8. discovered
9. discovery
10. archeological
11. archeologist
12. died
13. death

TUTANKHAMEN or **TUTENKHAMON** (About 1350 B.C.) an Egyptian king who ruled from the age of nine until his death at the age of eighteen. During his nine-year rule, he brought peace to his kingdom. But he is best known today because of his tomb, which Howard Carter and George Herbert discovered in 1922. When they found the tomb, it was filled with magnificent treasures, and it is now considered one of the greatest archeological discoveries of the twentieth century. (See Howard Carter, Egyptian history, George Herbert)

Image of Tutankhamen painted on his coffin

CARTER, HOWARD (1873-1939) British archeologist, born in London. Carter spent most of his time working in Egypt where he made several important discoveries. He is best known for his discovery of the tomb of King Tutankhamen, which he and George Herbert found in 1922. Inside this tomb they found magnificent treasures that are now in the Egyptian Museum in Cairo, Egypt. (See George Herbert, Tutankhamen)

HERBERT, GEORGE (1866-1923) The fifth Lord of Carnavon and Egyptologist, born near Newbury, England, and educated at the University of Cambridge. He traveled widely as a young man, and in 1903 he went to Egypt for the first time. He and Howard Carter are known especially for their discovery in Egypt of King Tutankhamen's tomb, which they opened on February 17, 1923. Two months later, Herbert died suddenly. Many people believed that his death was somehow caused by the opening of the tomb. (See Howard Carter, Tutankhamen)

The tomb of Tutankhamen as it appeared in 1922

Words

See pp. 76–77 for a list of present and past participles and p. 77 for a list of compass directions.

Help yourselves.	scenery	coast	can (n)	exactly	optimistic
go to (so much) trouble	park (n)	part	word (n)	located	strong
care for something	guide	chapter	couldn't (can)	spectacular	national
put something down	cliff dwelling	baby	hold	overpriced	
tourist	room	cookie	laugh (v)	historical	

11. Is it still available?

Lge 2 BR on quiet st nr transp. Avail immed. $500, unheated.
237-9462 eve.

Tired of city living? 1 BR apt in mod bldg, 10 mi N of town in lovely sub setting.
822-5470

3 rm mod apt, great loc. $450.
237-2483

1 BR apt nr buses. Reasonable rent.
786-5430

Try this

Trudy is looking for an a[...]
This is what she wants:

1. at least three rooms (living room, kitchen, bedroom) and a bath
2. rent #350 a month maximum, including heat
3. central location, near transportation
4. quiet street
5. not on first floor
6. modern building, if possible

**1. Read the ads. Then try to figure out what these abbreviations mean.
You will find the answers on p. 134.**

apt	bldg	lge	nr	st
avail	eve	loc	N	sub
BR	immed	mod	rm	transp

2. Now choose a partner and discuss these questions.

1. Which apartment is best for Trudy? Give reasons for your choice.
2. What questions will Trudy have to ask if she calls about the apartment?

A week later Trudy is still looking for an apartment, and her friend Hiro is helping her.

(A) ● Hiro
    ○ Trudy

- ● How does this sound? "Sunny one-bedroom near transportation, centrally located. . . ."
- ○ It's just what I'm looking for. Does it say how much it is?
- ● It's $450 a month including heat.
- ○ I can't pay that much.
- ● Maybe you should look for a roommate.
- ○ No, I'd rather have my own place. Now here's a one-bedroom for $350 a month on Oak Street. Do you have any idea where that is?
- ● It's off Washington, near the park.

● Hello?
○ Hello, I'm calling about the apartment you advertised. Is it still available?
● Yes, it is.
○ Could you tell me more about it?
● Well, there are three rooms and a bath.
○ How big are the rooms?
● The living room's fairly large—about eighteen feet by twenty-three feet. The bedroom and kitchen are kind of small. Oh, and there's parking available. Do you have a car?
○ Yes, but I'd rather not drive to work. How close is it to public transportation?
● There's a bus stop a block away.
○ Do you know what buses stop there?
● The number 1 and the number 2.
○ I could take the number 2 to work. Do you happen to know how often it runs during rush hour?
● Every five minutes or so.
○ It sounds perfect. What floor is it on?
● The first floor.
○ Hmm . . . that's a problem. I'd rather not live on the first floor.
● Well, that's all I have for the time being, but I will have a studio on the third floor in the near future.
○ How soon will it be available?
● November 1st.
○ Oh, well, I really can't wait that long. But thanks anyway.

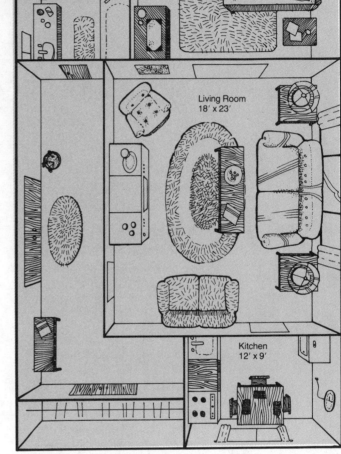

For other parts of a house, see p. 135.

Figure it out

1. Say *Right*, *Wrong*, or *I don't know.*

1. Trudy wants to live alone.   *Right.*
2. Trudy calls about a three-bedroom apartment.
3. Trudy doesn't drive.
4. Trudy needs an apartment before November 1st.
5. Washington Street is near the park.
6. The Oak Street apartment is $350 a month with heat.

2. Find another way to say it.

1. big   *large*
2. fairly small
3. now
4. very soon
5. about every five minutes

3. Match.

1. How soon?
2. How often?
3. How close?
4. How much?
5. How big?

a. Every ten minutes.
b. $350 a month.
c. November 1st.
d. Eighteen by twenty-three.
e. The next block.

Ways to say it

1 ASK WHERE A STREET IS

Ask about streets on the map and then about streets in your town.

● Do you | know / have any idea | where *Oak* Street is?

○ It's *off Washington, near the park.*　　○ No, (I'm afraid) I don't.

Some streets and locations	
Oak	off Oak
Washington	off Washington, near the park
Jefferson	parallel to Liberty
Liberty	parallel to Lincoln, on the other side of the park
Lincoln	parallel to Washington, on the other side of the park
Gate	crosses Washington
Pine	off Washington, not far from the park

2 TALK ABOUT TRANSPORTATION

● Do you know how often the number *1* bus runs *during rush hour?*

○ Oh, every *five* minutes or so.　　○ Sorry, I have no idea.

Some time periods
during rush hour
during the day
at night
on Saturday

Ways you've said it

about every five minutes

BUSES: approximate frequency in minutes

No.	Rush Hour	Day	Night	Sat.	Sun.
1	5	10	20	12	12
2	6	15	25	15	20
3	12	15	30	30	45
4	7	10	15	15	15

3 Ask how to get to different places in your town.

● Could you tell me what | bus / train | goes to *the Fine Arts Museum?*

○ Well, the number *1* stops *a block away.*　　○ I don't know. Sorry.

4 TALK ABOUT THE SIZE OF AN APARTMENT

First, play the role of the landlady and answer questions about the apartment that Trudy was interested in, using the floor plan on p. 83. Then pretend that you have advertised your own apartment in the newspaper.

● I'm calling about the apartment you advertised. Is it still available?

○ Yes, it is.
● Could you tell me how big the rooms are?
○ Well, the *living room's* (fairly large) about *eighteen* feet by *twenty-three* feet.
● And how big is the *kitchen? . . .*

○ No, I'm sorry, it's already rented.

1 foot = 0.30 meter

It's rented. = Someone rented it.

84

5 Close-up

INCLUDED QUESTIONS

Where **is** it?	
How much **does** it **cost**?	
How soon **will** it **be** available?	

Does it say	where it **is**?
Do you know	how much it **costs**?
Could you tell me	how soon it **will be** available?

Included subject questions

	What's playing at the State? What bus goes to the Fine Arts Museum?
Do you know Could you tell me	what's playing at the State? what bus goes to the Fine Arts Museum?

> When the question word is the *subject* of the included question, the word order is the same as in a simple subject question.

6 ASK ABOUT APARTMENTS

Practice the conversation below. Play Role A or Role B.

● How does this sound? *Sunny one-bedroom near transportation, centrally located....*
○ Does it say *how much it is?*

● *$450* a month.　　　● No, it doesn't.

Role A

You are helping a friend find an apartment in your neighborhood, and you see these ads in *Community News*, the local paper. Call your friend and suggest each of the apartments in the ads by reading the beginning of each ad. Then answer your friend's questions using the information in the ad.

- -

Role B

A friend is helping you find an apartment in his or her neighborhood and calls you after seeing some ads in *Community News*, the local paper. Respond to your friend's suggestions by asking each of the questions in the box below.

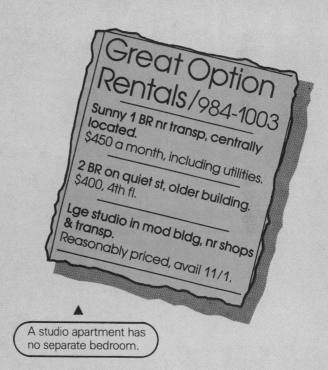

Great Option Rentals/984-1003

Sunny 1 BR nr transp, centrally located.
$450 a month, including utilities.

2 BR on quiet st, older building. $400, 4th fl.

Lge studio in mod bldg, nr shops & transp. Reasonably priced, avail 11/1.

▲

> A studio apartment has no separate bedroom.

Some questions
How much is it? What does the rent include? (What utilities are included?) Where is it (located)? What floor is it on? How close is it to transportation? How soon will it be available?

◀ utilities = heat (and hot water), gas, and electricity

7 ASK ABOUT APARTMENTS

**Now call Great Option Rentals about each
apartment in exercise 6 and ask the questions that
weren't answered in the ads. Another student will
answer your questions using the information on the
cards. Begin some of your questions with _Could you
please tell me . . . ?_**

- Great Option Rentals. May I help you?
- ○ Yes. I'm calling about the _one-bedroom_ apartment
  you advertised in <u>Community News</u>. Could you
  please tell me _where it is?_
- _It's on Crescent Street, off Park Drive._
- ○ And could you please tell me . . . ?

> One-bedroom: 348 Crescent St.
> Apt. 1A (off Park Drive)
>
> First floor. Available the first
> of the month. One block from bus.
> $450, including all utilities.

> Two-bedroom: 20 Maple St.
> Apt. 4 (off Grand Avenue)
> Rent includes heat, but other utili-
> ties extra. Available immediately.
> Fourth floor. 10-minute walk to
> nearest bus stop. $400.

> Studio: 413 Walnut St. Apt. 2B
>
> $200 a month, not including utili-
> ties. Heat, gas, and electricity
> extra. Second floor. Two blocks
> from buses and shops. Available
> 11/1.

8 STATE A PREFERENCE

**You work at Great Option Rentals, and someone calls you who is looking for a low-rent apartment. Suggest
each of the apartments below.**

- We have a _studio for $225 a month. It's in a modern building._

○ It sounds perfect. It's just what I'm
looking for.

○ I'd rather _live in an older building._
I'd rather not _live in a modern building._

Some apartments

a studio for $225 a month—in a modern building
a one-bedroom on the first floor—$325 a month
a studio near public transportation—$200 a
    month—on the top floor
a one-bedroom for $275 a month—in an older
    building about ten miles from town

Ways you've said it

I like old houses better.

It's _too_ far from town.
I'd rather not live _that_ far from town.

I'd rather . . . =
I would rather . . .

9 Close-up

I'D RATHER AND I'D RATHER NOT

I'd rather	live in an older building. have a one-bedroom.
I'd rather not	live in a modern building. pay that much.

It's not quite what I had in mind.

Doug is telling Luke Hopper and Gloria Smith about his new apartment at Gloria's going-away party. Luke is originally from England. 🔲

1

Luke: So Kate tells me you found a flat.*

Doug: Yes, as a matter of fact, she's the one who told me about it. A friend of hers lives in the same building.

Luke: What's it like?

Doug: It's a studio—one big room with a kitchenette. I'd rather have a one-bedroom, but at the prices they're asking, I can't afford it, at least not for the time being.

Gloria: I know what you mean. Apartments cost an arm and a leg these days. I hope we can find something inexpensive in Madison. Is it in pretty good shape at least?

Doug: Yes. They've renovated the whole building. Actually, it's not quite what I had in mind. I like more modern places, but I'm lucky to have found this. And the location's great.

Luke: Where is it exactly?

Doug: On Wilson, right off Broadway.

Luke: Oh, yes. I know where that is. That *is* a good location. Are you all moved in and settled?

Doug: For the most part. The walls are kind of bare, though. Does either of you know where I can get some posters around here?

Luke: Not offhand.

Gloria: Ask Kate. She'd know that kind of thing.

*In British English, the word *flat* is used instead of *apartment*.

2. Figure it out

Say *Right, Wrong,* or *I don't know.*

1. Doug looked for an apartment for a long time and found just what he wanted.   *Wrong.*
2. Doug thinks the rents in Chicago are expensive.
3. Doug doesn't have enough money for a one-bedroom apartment.
4. Luke has lived in Chicago for a few years.
5. Gloria is going to move out of Chicago.
6. Doug hasn't moved into his new apartment yet.
7. The apartment is in a new building.

3 Listen in 🔲

Gloria is telling Mr. Dow and Kate Simmons about her future plans. Read the questions below. Then listen to the conversation and choose *a* or *b*.

1. Why are Gloria and her husband, John, moving to Madison?
   a. John has a new job.
   b. Gloria is going back to school.

2. How soon do Gloria and John have to be in Madison?
   a. In about two weeks.
   b. In a few days.

Your turn

Where do you think each of these homes is
located—in the city, the suburbs, or the country?

Valerie Dumont

Elaine and
David Keller

Joan and
Harry Robinson

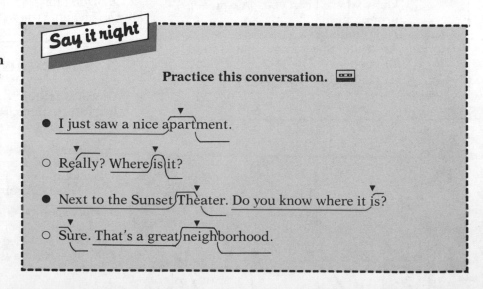

Which home do you think is best
for the people above? Why? Which
home would you like to live in the
most? Why? Discuss these
questions in groups.

On your own

What determines the kind of home we live in?

One of the things that strikes people who travel is that homes look so different from one place to another. Yet three factors — climate, available building materials, and lifestyle — usually decide the kind of housing a place will have.

People build homes that will protect them from bad weather and let them enjoy good weather. In very wet countries like Thailand and Malaysia, homes are often built high off the ground to protect them from floods. Where the weather is very hot, as in the deserts of Australia, or very cold, as in the Arctic, people sometimes live underground, away from the outside. In places where the weather is mild, homes often have courtyards that are open to the sky. This type of home is common in Spain and in parts of Latin America. Some Middle Eastern countries, such as Iran, have homes with thick walls that keep people warm in the winter and cool in the summer.

Homes are built from materials that are easily available, and sometimes these can be very unusual. In hot, dry places such as the southwestern United States, people often use mud to build homes because wood is hard to find. In Coober Pedy, Australia, where there are many opal mines, some people live in underground caves with opal walls. The Eskimos of the Arctic often live in temporary houses of snow when they go on hunting trips.

Perhaps people's lifestyles are more obvious in their homes than anywhere else. Most of us think of a home as a permanent place, but the Bedouins of North Africa and the Middle East, who travel from one location to another, often live in tents that they can carry with them. In parts of Indonesia, where parents, children, grandparents, aunts, and uncles all live together, people build homes called "longhouses" and add rooms when necessary. Some Middle Eastern homes have two living rooms, one for guests and the other for the family.

Homes not only offer shelter, but are a key to the culture and way of life of a people. For this reason, they have always fascinated historians and other scholars.

Pueblo homes in New Mexico made of mud bricks

Bedouin tents in northeastern Iran

Read the magazine article. Then answer these questions.

1. Why are houses built high off the ground in Thailand? *To protect them from floods.*
2. Why do people sometimes live underground in Australia?
3. Why do houses in Iran have thick walls?
4. Why do people use mud to build houses in the southwestern part of the United States?
5. Why do the Bedouins live in tents?
6. Why do people in Indonesia build "longhouses"?

Words

See the floor plan on p. 83 for a list of some rooms in a house.

Could you tell me . . .?	not far from	rent (n)	shop (n)	include	off
Does it say . . .?	a block away	rented (adj)	studio (apartment)	available	centrally
have any/no idea	How close . . .?	utilities	cross (v)	perfect	or so
I'd rather (not) . . .	How soon . . .?	heat (n)	run	public (adj)	
on the other side of	rush hour	gas	advertise	top (adj)	
	transportation	electricity	sound (v)	parallel to	

12. It depends . . .

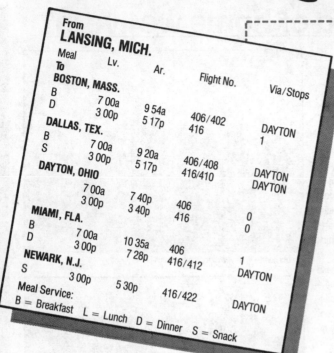

From **LANSING, MICH.**				
Meal	Lv.	Ar.	Flight No.	Via/Stops
To				
BOSTON, MASS.				
B	7 00a	9 54a	406/402	
D	3 00p	5 17p	416	DAYTON
				1
DALLAS, TEX.				
B	7 00a	9 20a	406/408	DAYTON
S	3 00p	5 17p	416/410	DAYTON
DAYTON, OHIO				
	7 00a	7 40p	406	0
	3 00p	3 40p	416	0
MIAMI, FLA.				
B	7 00a	10 35a	406	1
D	3 00p	7 28p	416/412	DAYTON
NEWARK, N.J.				
S	3 00p	5 30p	416/422	DAYTON

Meal Service:
B = Breakfast   L = Lunch   D = Dinner   S = Snack

Look at the timetable. All of the flights leave from Lansing, Michigan. Then choose a partner and discuss these questions.

1. What time does Flight 416 leave Lansing? What time does it arrive in Dayton, Ohio?
2. How long does it take to get from Lansing to Miami, Florida?
3. To get from Lansing to Newark, New Jersey, you have to change planes in Dayton. On which flight—416 or 422—do they serve a snack?
4. Is there a direct flight* from Lansing to Dallas, Texas?
5. Does the morning flight from Lansing to Miami make a stop or is it nonstop?
6. There are two flights a day between Lansing and Boston. Which one is better in your opinion? Why?
7. Do they serve any meals on Flight 406 to Miami?

*You don't have to change planes on a direct flight.

Bob Ross and Ann Watson, who live in Lansing, Michigan, are talking about their plans for the long holiday weekend.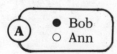

(A)
- ● Bob
- ○ Ann

- ● Any plans for the long weekend?
- ○ It depends on the weather. If it's nice, I'll probably go camping. But if it isn't, maybe I'll just stay home and clean my apartment. It could certainly use it. How about you?
- ● I'm going to Dayton.
- ○ Oh, is that where you're from?
- ● No, that's where my parents live now. I grew up in Delaware.

- ○ How are you getting there?
- ● I'm thinking of flying, but it depends on how much it costs. If it's too expensive, I'll take the bus.
- ○ Well, listen, if you need a ride to the airport, let me know. I'll be happy to take you, if I'm around.
- ● Oh, thanks. That's really nice of you.

	● Bob
B	○ Mr. Ross
	▲ Mrs. Ross

○ Hello?

● Hello, Dad?

○ Bob! We've been expecting your call. *(To his wife)* It's Bob.

▲ Find out when he's coming.

○ When are you coming?

● Saturday at four.

○ *(To his wife)* He's coming on Saturday at four.

▲ Not until four? How come?

○ Why so late?

● I couldn't get an earlier flight.

○ *(To his wife)* He couldn't get an earlier flight.

● Have you heard from Carol?

○ Have I heard what?

● Have you heard from Carol?

○ Yes. She can't come until Saturday night. She couldn't get the day off at the hospital.

● Oh, that's too bad.

○ Bob, I can hardly hear what you're saying. Could you speak a little louder?

● I said that's too bad. Listen, this is a terrible connection. Give my love to Mom and I'll see you both on Saturday.

○ O.K., I will. See you Saturday.

Figure it out

1. Say *Right*, *Wrong*, or *I don't know*.

1. Ann is going camping over the long weekend. *I don't know.*
2. Bob is from Dayton.
3. Bob is going to fly to Dayton.

4. Mr. Ross couldn't hear Bob because the telephone wasn't working well.
5. Carol is Bob's sister.
6. Carol has to work on Saturday.

2. Choose *a* or *b*.

1. Find out _____ .
   a. when is he coming
   ⓑ when he's coming

2. It depends on _____ .
   a. how long does it take
   b. how long it takes

3. If _____ a ride, let me know.
   a. you need
   b. you'll need

4. I tried to get an earlier flight, _____ .
   a. but I can't
   b. but I couldn't

91

Ways to say it

1 (TALK ABOUT PLANS)

- Do you have any plans for the weekend?
- ○ It depends on the weather. If it's nice, I'll (probably) go camping, but if it isn't (nice), I'll . . .

What if . . .?	Some things to do in bad weather

it's nice
it isn't (nice)
it rains
it doesn't (rain)
it snows
it doesn't (snow)
	run errands:
	  go to the bank/dry cleaners
	  go grocery shopping
	stay home and clean the house
	stay home and get some work
	  done
	catch up on some reading

2 (MAKE AN OFFER)

- I hear you're flying to Columbus this weekend.
- ○ Yes, I am. (I'm leaving Friday night after work.)
- Well, listen, if you need a ride to the airport, I'll be happy to take you.

A friend is . . .	You offer to . . .

flying to Columbus and might
  need a ride to the airport.
moving into a new apartment and
  might need help.
going camping and might need
  to borrow a tent.
	take her.
	
	come over and
	  give him a hand.
	lend him yours.

3  CONDITIONAL SENTENCES

	Present tense	Future tense
If	the weather is good, it isn't too cold,	we'll have a picnic. I'll go to the beach.
	it rains, it doesn't clear up,	we won't go camping. I won't go shopping.

4 Complete each statement using personal information.

1. If it's nice this weekend, _I'll go to the beach_ .
2. If I don't have much work tonight, _____ .
3. _____ , I'll answer some letters.
4. _____ , I probably won't go out this weekend.
5. If it doesn't rain tomorrow, _____ .

6. If I can save enough money, _____ .
7. _____ , I'll stay home and read a book.
8. If I learn to speak English fluently, _____ .

5 (TALK ABOUT A TRIP)

- I'm going to Dayton for the weekend.
- ○ Oh, really? How are you getting there?
- I'm thinking of flying, but it depends on how much it costs. If it's too expensive, I'll take the bus.

  ▲

It depends on how much it costs is an included question.

Some questions
How much does it cost? (How much is it?) How long does it take? (How long is the trip?) What time does the flight (train, bus) leave?

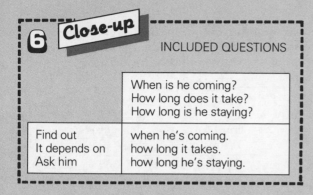

6 INCLUDED QUESTIONS

	When is he coming? How long does it take? How long is he staying?
Find out It depends on Ask him	when he's coming. how long it takes. how long he's staying.

7 You have just gone away to college and you're calling home for the first time. Two students will play the roles of your mother and father, and one will talk to you on the phone while the other says what questions to ask. Answer their questions using personal information.

● *Ask her how she's feeling.*
○ *How are you feeling, Sue?*
▲ *I'm feeling fine.*
● *Find out . . .*

Some questions
How is she feeling? What classes is he taking? How does she like her classes? What's the weather like? When is he coming home?

Ask her how she's feeling.

8 GIVE AN EXCUSE

You have plans to visit a friend in another city, and you call to say you'll be arriving later than you planned. Begin the conversation any way you wish, but end it like this:

● When are you coming?
○ *Saturday* at *four.*
● Not until *four?* How come?
○ I couldn't *get an earlier flight.*

Some excuses	
I couldn't	get an earlier flight. get a reservation for Friday night. find a baby-sitter for Friday night. get Friday afternoon off.

9 ASK FOR CLARIFICATION

Think of a question to ask another student. He or she will answer using personal information.

● *Have you finished the homework?*
○ Could you speak a little *louder?*
● *HAVE YOU FINISHED THE HOMEWORK? . . .*

Could you speak . . . ?
louder slower more clearly

10 Close-up

THE COMPARATIVE OF ADVERBS

Can you come a little	sooner?
I'll try to drive	more carefully.

One syllable	More than one syllable
Adverb + er	More or less + adverb

▲

But:
well ▶ better
badly ▶ worse
early ▶ earlier

11

Read the information for each item. Then respond appropriately using the comparative form of one of the adverbs in the box.

badly	fast	often	well
carefully	late	slow (or	
clearly	loud (or	slowly)	
early	loudly)	soon	

1. Someone tells you that you speak English well. You think you've forgotten a lot. Talk about the past.

I used to speak English better.

2. Someone is speaking very fast, and you can't understand him. Make a request.

3. You're supposed to go out with a friend at 7:00, and it's already 6:30. You haven't finished your work yet, so you call your friend. Make a suggestion.

4. A friend asks you to come over right away. It takes you a long time to get there because there's a lot of traffic. Apologize and give an excuse.

5. Someone fills out a form for you. You can't read her name or her address. Make a request.

12 MAKE RESERVATIONS

Act out the conversation. Play Role A or Role B.

Role A

You live in Lansing, Michigan, and you want to take a trip to Miami, Florida. Call Piedmont Airlines and ask for information about flights to Miami. First, find out how long each flight takes. Then choose a flight and make a reservation. You may use these expressions: *I'd rather (not) . . ., change planes,* and *nonstop.*

Role B

You work at the reservations desk of Piedmont Airlines, and someone calls about flights from Lansing, Michigan, to Miami, Florida. Answer his or her questions using the timetable on p. 90. Be sure to give information about both flights. You may use these expressions: *It depends on . . . direct, makes a stop,* and *takes longer.*

Start like this:
● *Piedmont Airlines. May I help you?*
○ *Yes, I'd like some information about flights from Lansing to Miami. Could you please tell me . . . ?*

I was just wondering . . .

Terry Enders has just knocked at Doug Lee's door. 🔳

1

Terry: Hi! My name's Terry Enders. I'm Kate's friend.

Doug: Oh, hi, Terry. I'm Doug Lee. You live upstairs, right?

Terry: That's right, in the apartment above yours. . . . Mmm, something smells delicious. Are you cooking?

Doug: Well, it depends on what you call cooking. I'm just making some chicken . . . very basic. Uh, would you like to come in?

Terry: Oh, thanks, no, I don't want to disturb you. I was just wondering if you knew Kate's new phone number. I can't seem to find it.

Doug: Uh, no, I don't. But if you call the old one, there'll probably be a recording telling you the new one.

Terry: Oh, you know, you're right. I don't know why I didn't think of that. . . .

Doug: You know, it's the funniest thing. . . . Your name sounded really familiar when Kate first mentioned you, and now that I see you, you look familiar, too. We haven't met somewhere before, have we?

Terry: No, I don't think so. You're probably confusing me with my sister. She's pretty well known.

Doug: Oh? Who is she? (*Phone rings upstairs*)

Terry: Oh, listen, that's my phone. I'll talk to you later, O.K.? (*Calling down from upstairs*) Nice meeting you!

Doug: Nice meeting you, too. . . .

2. Figure it out

Say *Right*, *Wrong*, or *I don't know*.

1. Doug invites Terry to dinner.   *Wrong.*
2. Terry's sister is a well-known actress.
3. Doug suggests that Terry call Kate's old number to find out her new one.
4. Doug thinks that maybe he's seen Terry before.
5. Terry runs upstairs to answer her phone.

3. Listen in 🔳

Terry gets a phone call from Laura, who tells her that Chuck is in Portland, Oregon. Read the statements below. Then listen to the phone conversation and choose *a* or *b*.

1. Chuck is still in Portland because _____ .
   a. he couldn't get a flight back
   b. he decided to stay longer

2. If Chuck isn't back in time for dinner, _____ .
   a. Laura won't go to Terry's
   b. Laura will go to Terry's alone

Your turn

What should you do if you are ever in one of these situations? Discuss this question in groups. Try to think of as many different possibilities as you can.

If you're ever in a fire, you should try to stay calm. . . .

Have you ever been in a dangerous situation like these? If you have, tell what happened and what you did.

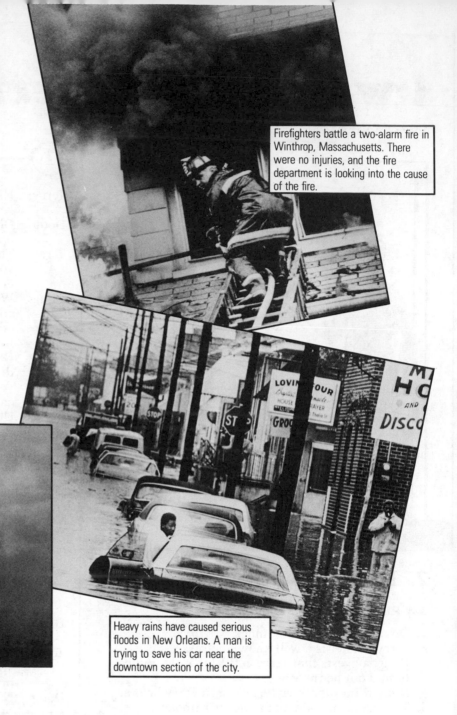

Firefighters battle a two-alarm fire in Winthrop, Massachusetts. There were no injuries, and the fire department is looking into the cause of the fire.

Heavy rains have caused serious floods in New Orleans. A man is trying to save his car near the downtown section of the city.

Once again a tornado has hit the midwestern part of the United States. Twenty people are known to be dead outside Marshallton, Iowa, and property damage will probably reach 5 million dollars.

Say it right

Practice this conversation. 📼

● If it's nice, I'll go camping this weekend.

○ It's supposed to be. If it isn't too hot, maybe I'll go to the beach.

On your own

Over Two Thousand Years of Weather Forecasts

Satellite photo of twin hurricanes

More than once you have probably listened to a weather report, heard a prediction for a warm, sunny day, and then got caught in a storm without an umbrella. If you think that this happens to you often, it may surprise you to know that a one-day weather forecast is actually about 87 percent accurate.

Weather forecasting is a precise science. In the Northern Hemisphere alone, there are about two thousand weather stations. These stations send out their reports four times a day, seven days a week.

Today meteorologists, or people who study the weather, use satellites with instruments to measure temperature. These satellites also have cameras which photograph the land and sea. The United Nations' World Meteorological Organization is working to make weather predictions even more accurate, but it will probably be a long time before 100-percent accuracy is possible.

Weather forecasting began as early as the fifth century B.C. Scientists started to make predictions about the direction of the wind, an important help to sailors. Aristotle and his student Theophrastus also wrote about ways to predict the weather. The studies of Theophrastus remained important for the next two thousand years. Amazingly, scientists have found that his most important predictions were correct around 70 percent of the time.

Before the seventeenth century, there were no scientific instruments to study the weather. In 1643 the barometer, which measures air pressure, was invented. The thermometer, which measures temperature, and the hygroscope, which tells you the humidity, or the amount of water in the air, soon followed. Scientists also started to keep records of the weather in the seventeenth century, and this helped them to understand how weather patterns repeated. Scientists then began to pass on their discoveries to those in other countries, making meteorology an international science.

1. Read the magazine article. Then say *Right* or *Wrong*.

1. The first weather predictions were made in the fifteenth century B.C. *Wrong.*
2. Early weather predictions helped sailors.
3. The weather predictions of Theophrastus were almost never correct.
4. Satellites were invented before the barometer.
5. Today a one-day prediction is about 87 percent accurate.
6. Soon scientists will be able to give us weather reports that are 100 percent accurate.

2. Find definitions in the article for these words.

1. meteorologist   *someone who studies the weather*
2. humidity
3. barometer
4. thermometer
5. hygroscope

Words

See p. 94 for a list of adverbs taught in this unit.

reading (n)	reservation	How come?	get (time) off	serve
dry cleaners	baby-sitter	It depends on . . .	run errands	calm
airport	snack	Find out . . .	catch up on	direct (adj)
tent	flood	get some work done	fly	nonstop
flight	tornado	give someone a hand	change (v)	if

13. This must be a

Are you ready to order?

1. Look at the menu. Then act out this conversation.

You and three friends are having dinner at The Brass Lantern. Talk about what you're going to order. Find out who has eaten there before and ask for suggestions. Here are some expressions you can use: *I might . . . , I'm thinking of . . . , I think I'll . . . , I haven't decided yet,* and *either . . . or. . . .*

2. Now choose a fifth student to be the waiter or waitress, and then give your order.

The Brass Lantern

DINNERS

All dinners come with soup, choice of salad or fresh vegetable, potatoes (baked or French fried) or rice, and coffee or tea.

Broiled Jumbo Shrimp with Garlic Sauce	$11.95
Chicken "Brass Lantern"	$8.95
Sirloin Steak	$14.95
Filet of Sole with Almonds	$10.95
Liver and Onions	$9.95

A
- ● Joe
- ○ Janet
- ▲ Meg
- △ Mike
- ■ Waiter

Four friends are trying a new restaurant. 📼

● Hey, look at that crowd! This must be a great place to eat!
○ It's a good thing we made a reservation.
▲ I know just what I want—shrimp with garlic sauce.
○ Mmm, that sounds good. You know, I think I might have that, too.
▲ Do you know what you're getting, Mike?
△ I can't make up my mind. I can't decide between the shrimp and the steak.
▲ Oh, get the shrimp. You can always get a steak.
■ Are you ready to order?
▲ Yes, I'll have the shrimp, please.
■ I'm sorry, there's no more shrimp. . . .

great place!

B

▲ Everything looks delicious!
△ Uh, this isn't mine. I ordered steak—well done.
■ Oh, I'm really sorry. I'll bring your steak right away.
● Do you mind if we start?
△ Oh, no, please do.
○ Oh, waiter, could I have another fork, please? This one isn't clean.
● And could we have some more water, please?
■ Certainly.
△ Does anyone mind if I smoke?
○ Well . . . actually, I'd rather you didn't.
△ Oh, well, no problem. How's your fish, Meg?
▲ It tastes kind of funny to me. Here, taste it.
△ Uh, no thanks. Why don't you send it back and get something else?
▲ Good idea. I think I'll get a steak.

C

△ Listen to that song! Do you know what it is?
● Hmm, it sounds familiar, but I don't remember what it's called.
▲ It's "Smoke Gets in Your Eyes."
○ Speaking of smoke, I smell smoke—don't you?
▲ It must be a cigar. It smells awful.
○ No, I think it's coming from the kitchen. (*Starts coughing*)
■ Your steak, sir. (*To Meg*) Yours will be here in a few minutes, ma'am.
△ Well, it *is* well done.

Figure it out

1. Say *Right*, *Wrong*, or *I don't know*.

1. The waiter brought Mike the wrong order. *Right*.
2. Everyone started eating at the same time.
3. Mike doesn't smoke.
4. Everyone wanted to order shrimp.
5. Meg ordered fish because they were out of shrimp.
6. Meg sent her fish back and ordered chicken.

2. Match.

1. My fork isn't clean.
2. We're out of water.
3. Listen to that song.
4. I smell smoke.
5. Do you mind if I start?

a. I'll bring you some more.
b. No, please do.
c. Yes, I do. Please do.
d. It sounds familiar.
e. I'll bring you another one.
f. It must be a cigar.

Ways to say it

1 STATE A CONCLUSION

- Look at that *crowd! This* must be *a great place to eat!*
- It's a good thing *we made a reservation*.

Look at that . . .	Some conclusions	It's a good thing . . .
crowd. line. traffic.	There's an accident up ahead. This is a great place to eat. This is a popular movie.	we made a reservation. we're not very hungry. we left home early. we're not in a hurry. we already have tickets.

crowd

line

traffic

2 TALK ABOUT WHAT YOU'RE ORDERING

Use the menu on p. 98.

- Do you know what you're going to order?

I'm going to get the *chicken*.	Well, the *shrimp with garlic sauce* sounds good. I think I might get that.

- How about you? . . .

I can't make up my mind. I haven't decided yet.

I can't decide between the *shrimp* and the *steak*.

3 REQUEST SOMETHING

- Could I have another *piece of pie*, / some more *pie*, please?
- Certainly. I'll get it for you right away. Anything else for you, *sir?*
  - Yes. Could you bring me . . . ?
  - No, thanks. Just the check.

You've already had . . .

(a piece of) pie/cake.
(a cup of) coffee/tea.
(a glass of) milk/water.
bread.
rolls.
butter.

Count nouns	Mass nouns
another roll some more rolls	some more butter

4 Close-up

ANOTHER, SOME (ANY) MORE, AND SOMETHING (ANYTHING) ELSE

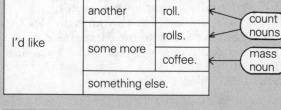

	another	roll.
I'd like	some more	rolls.
		coffee.
	something else.	

count nouns → roll. / rolls.
mass noun → coffee.

	another	roll.
I don't want	any more	rolls.
		coffee.
	anything else.	

another roll ▶ another *one*
some more coffee ▶ some more

5 You've invited a friend over for dinner. Her plate is empty, and there's a lot of food left on the table. Fill in the blanks with *another (one)*, *some (any) more*, or *something (anything) else*. There may be more than one answer.

- How about _another_ piece of chicken, Sally?
- ○ No, thanks. It was delicious, but I've already eaten too much.
- Are you sure? There's still a little salad. Why don't you have _____ ?
- ○ No, really, I can't eat _____ thing.
- Well, then, can I get you _____ to drink?
- ○ Well, maybe I will have _____ glass of water.

(*During dessert*)

- ○ These cookies are terrific!
- Well, here, have _____ .
- ○ Oh, I really shouldn't eat _____ , but maybe I will have _____ .

6 ⬭ ASK PERMISSION

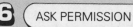

● Do you mind if I *smoke*?

○ Oh, no, | not at all. / please do. | ○ Well, I'd rather you didn't.

Ways you've said it
- May I smoke?
- ○ Go right ahead.

You'd like to . . .
smoke.
open the window.
close the window.
turn on the radio.
turn off the radio.

7 ⬭ ASK HOW SOMEONE'S FOOD IS

● How's your *fish*?

○ *Delicious.* Would you like to taste it?
● *Sure.*

○ It tastes *kind of funny*.
● Why don't you send it back and get something else? . . .

It tastes . . .
delicious.
pretty good.
kind of funny/strange.
spoiled.
awful.

8 ⬭ IDENTIFY A SONG

● Listen to this song. (*Hum part of a song.*) Do you know what it is?

○ It's "*Smoke Gets in Your Eyes.*"

○ It sounds familiar, but I don't remember what it's called.

○ I've never heard it before.

Compare *listen* and *hear:*
Listen to this record.
Turn up the volume. I can't hear it.

9 ⬭ IDENTIFY A PERSON

You may look up the answers to this exercise on p. 134.

● Do you know who this is?

○ *Humphrey Bogart.*

○ *He* looks familiar, but I'm not sure who *he* is.

○ I've never seen *him* before.

Compare *look* and *see:*
Look at these pictures.
Turn on the light. I can't see them.

Close-up

10 SENSE VERBS

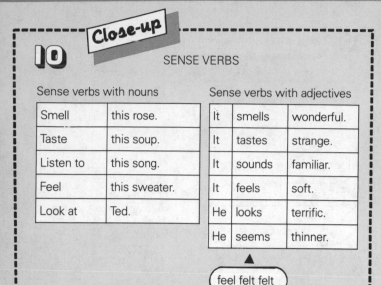

Sense verbs with nouns	
Smell	this rose.
Taste	this soup.
Listen to	this song.
Feel	this sweater.
Look at	Ted.

Sense verbs with adjectives		
It	smells	wonderful.
It	tastes	strange.
It	sounds	familiar.
It	feels	soft.
He	looks	terrific.
He	seems	thinner.

▲
feel felt felt

11 Fill in the blanks with appropriate sense verbs. Make sure to put them in the right tense.

1. ● I _smell_ onions.
   ○ It's this soup I'm making.
   ● Mmm . . . it _____ great.
   ○ Here, _____ it.
   ● Hmm, it _____ familiar.
   ○ That's because it's your mother's recipe.

2. ● _____ Al. His face is all red.
   ○ You're right. He really _____ awful. (*Walking over to Al*) Are you O.K., Al?
   ▲ Well, I _____ very well. (*Coughs*)
   ○ _____ that cough. It _____ terrible. I really think you should go home.

3. ● Have you seen Al?
   ○ He just went home. He wasn't _____ well.
   ● I know he had a terrible cough. It _____ pretty bad.
   ○ And he _____ terrible, too. I think he had a fever.

12 TALK ABOUT WHERE YOU'VE SEEN SOMEONE

Act out the conversation. Play Role A or Role B.

Role A

Another student looks very familiar, and you think you've seen him or her before. Try to figure out where, using this information about your own activities:

You swim at the university pool.
You work at Jack's Coffee Shop part-time.
You study at the university library.

Start like this:
● *You look very familiar. Have I seen you somewhere before?*
○ *You look familiar to me, too. Do you ever swim . . . ?*

End like this:
● *Then that's where we've seen each other!*

Role B

A student who looks familiar thinks you look familiar, too. Try to figure out where you've seen each other. Ask questions about his or her activities, using this information about your own:

You go folk dancing a lot.
You're taking a French class at the Adult Education Center.
You're a librarian at the university library.

Were you in Hong Kong in the summer of '81?

I've been thinking . . .

Laura goes to the airport to meet Chuck, who has just come back from a job interview in Portland, Oregon.

1

Chuck: You look happy. Are you glad to see me?

Laura: (*Laughs*) Well, you look happy, too! You seem much more relaxed.

Chuck: Yeah, I was pretty depressed for a while. It was nice to get away for a few days. But it's nice to be back, too.

Laura: So, tell me about the interview. How did it go?

Chuck: It went well. . . . As a matter of fact, it went very well. They offered me the job.

Laura: Oh . . . well, that's terrific. You must feel really good about it. Are you . . . uh . . . thinking of accepting it?

Chuck: I haven't told them yet. I have until Friday to let them know. I can't make up my mind. I love Chicago and, of course, you're here. You know how I feel about that. But this is the best opportunity I've ever had.

Laura: It sounds as if you've already made up your mind.

Chuck: Hey, don't look so sad. You know, I've been thinking a lot these last few days. This will probably sound crazy to you. . . . I mean, I know you have your sister and your friends and your job here, but I'd like you to go with me. . . . Listen, Laura, why don't we get married?

Laura: Chuck . . . do you mind if I sit down for a minute?

2. Figure it out

Say *Right*, *Wrong*, or *I don't know*.

1. Chuck has been in Portland for four days.
   I don't know.
2. Chuck was depressed before his trip.
3. Chuck has decided to take the job, but he hasn't accepted it yet.
4. Chuck wants Laura to marry him.
5. Laura wants to sit down because her feet are killing her.

3. Listen in

The next day at work, Laura has something else on her mind. Listen to the conversation. What two things did she forget?

Your turn

You are at the International Soup Café. Read about the soups on the menu. Then act out this conversation in groups of three. Two students will play the roles of customers, and one will play the role of a waiter or waitress.

Discuss the different soups and decide which one to order. If you have ever had any of these soups, make a recommendation. Then give the waiter or waitress your order.

The International Soup Café adds a new soup to its menu every month. What soup do you think they should add this month? Recommend a soup that's popular in your country, and describe it to your classmates.

"We have soups from all over the world."

Beid bi lamoun	A Middle Eastern chicken soup made with eggs, lemon, and rice. Served with buttered toast.
Won Ton Soup	A soup from China. Dumplings stuffed with pork served in a delicious broth.
Minestrone Soup	An Italian soup made with garden fresh vegetables and beans. Topped with Parmesan cheese. Served with Italian bread.
Vichyssoise	A wonderful hot weather soup from France. Made with leeks, potatoes, chicken broth, and cream. Served cold with French bread.
Gazpacho	A cold Spanish soup made from tomatoes, onions, cucumbers, green peppers, garlic, vinegar, olive oil, and bread. The name is Arabic for "soaked bread."
Chicken Gumbo Soup	From New Orleans. A soup made from chicken, tomatoes, onions, peppers, okra, and other fresh vegetables. Served with black bread.

All of our soups are $5.95 and come with salad, coffee, and dessert.

Say it right

Say the phrases below. Then practice the conversation.

would you [wújuw]
could you [kújuw]
why don't you [way dónčuw]

- Could you pass the salt? This soup has no taste.
- Would you like to taste my gazpacho? It's delicious.
- Oh, it *is* good.
- Why don't you order some?
- I think I will. I'm sorry I didn't order gazpacho before.

On your own

1. Read the ad. Then answer these questions.

1. What food helps you see better? *Carrots.*
2. Why is milk good for you?
3. What did your mother say you should eat every day?
4. What important vitamin does Campbell's Bean with Bacon Soup have?
5. What often happens when your resistance is low?
6. How does soup play an important part in a well-balanced diet?

2. Find another way to say it.

1. If you eat an apple a day, you won't have to go to the doctor. *An apple a day keeps the doctor away.*
2. Nutrition is important to good health.
3. For example, there's Campbell's Bean with Bacon Soup.
4. Low resistance often makes you get sick.

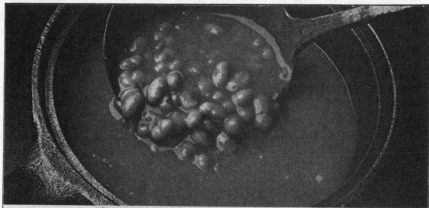

CAMPBELL'S SOUP. BETTER THAN AN APPLE A DAY.

Remember all those wonderful little sayings your mother had about food?

"Carrots help you see in the dark." "Milk gives you strong bones." "An apple a day keeps the doctor away."

She was on the right track. Common sense told her good nutrition plays an important part in good health.

And when she said, "Eat your soup, it's good for you," she was years ahead of her time.

CAMPBELL'S SOUP IS GOOD FOOD.

In a recent study of government data, university researchers found that soup can play a significant part in a healthy, well-balanced diet.

Take Campbell's Bean with Bacon Soup. Calorie for calorie, it's more nutritionally balanced than an apple. Besides supplying major nutrients like vitamin A, it also contains several essential "trace elements."

And soup doesn't just outshine an apple. There really aren't many foods that can match it for nutritional variety.

GOOD FOOD HELPS KEEP YOU HEALTHY.

Your chances of getting sick are higher when your resistance is low. But eating a balanced diet of good nutritious food, like soup, can help keep your resistance up.

So think about it. When was the last time you had some delicious, hot soup?

(And, by the way, when was the last time you called your mother?)

SOUP IS GOOD FOOD

Words

See p. 102 for a list of sense verbs.

make up one's mind	traffic	pie	folk dancing	spoiled
Do you mind if . . .?	garlic	recipe	smoke (n, v)	familiar
I'd rather you didn't.	sauce	song	send back	certainly
kind of	shrimp	pool	popular	ahead
crowd	piece	check (n)	strange	

14. There aren't many left.

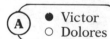

Try this

1. **Read the label on the cough medicine bottle. Then find another way to say these expressions:**

1. doctor
2. no more than
3. in twenty-four hours
4. older than eleven
5. amount to take
6. ask the advice of

DOSAGE:
Adults and children 12 years of age and over: 2 teaspoonfuls every four hours, not to exceed 12 teaspoonfuls in a 24-hour period. Children 6 to under 12 years: 1 teaspoonful every four hours, not to exceed 6 teaspoonfuls in a 24-hour period. Children 2 to under 6 years: ½ teaspoonful every four hours, not to exceed 3 teaspoonfuls in a 24-hour period. Children under 2 years: consult your physician.
Do not exceed recommended dosage.

2. **Act out the conversation. Play Role A or Role B.**

Role A

You have a headache and are looking for the aspirin, but you can't find it. Ask your brother if he knows where it is.

Role B

Your sister has a headache, but she can't find the aspirin. You're not sure where it is, either. Suggest different places around the house where she can look.

Dolores Duran isn't feeling well. She and her husband, Victor, have just gotten home from work. 📼

(A) ● Victor
○ Dolores

● Hi! Sorry I'm late. I got caught in traffic.
○ I just got home myself.
● Hey, you don't look very good.
○ I must be getting a cold. I've had this terrible headache since I got up, and I've been snee . . . A-A-ATCHOO! . . . sneezing all day.
● Bless you.
○ Thank you.
● Look, why don't you go upstairs and lie down? I'll bring you some aspirin.

B

- I don't see any aspirin in the medicine cabinet.
- ○ We must not have any more.
- Oh, wait, here's the bottle, behind the cough medicine. Hmm, there aren't many left. I'll go to the drugstore. Is there anything else we need?
- ○ Could you get some more ti . . . ATCHOO! . . . tissues? There are only a few left in the box. ATCHOO!
- Bless you.
- ○ Thank you. Oh, and could you get some more tea? We just ran out of tea bags.
- Any special kind?
- ○ No, I don't care.
- Now what did I do with my car keys?
- ○ Take mine. They're in my purse.
- Where's your purse?
- ○ It must be downstairs. Look on the kitchen table. If it's not there, it might be on the coffee table in the living room.

C
- Victor
- ○ Pharmacist

- Could you tell me where the tissues are, please?
- ○ All the way in the back, against the wall. *(A few minutes later)* Have you found them? They're way up on top.
- Oh, yes, I see them.

D

- Do you have tonight's paper?
- ○ We may not have any more. If there are any left, they're up in front with the magazines.
- I've already looked there.
- ○ Well, we must be out of them then.

Figure it out

1. Say *Right*, *Wrong*, or *I don't know*.

1. Dolores has been home for an hour. *Wrong.*
2. Dolores took two aspirin at work.
3. Victor and Dolores are all out of aspirin.
4. Victor and Dolores are all out of tea bags.
5. Victor left his car keys at the office.

2. Find another way to say it.

1. I just got home, too. *I just got home myself.*
2. I'm probably getting a cold.
3. Do we need anything else?
4. Maybe we're out of them.
5. We're probably out of them.

3. Fill in the blanks with *tea* or *tea bags*. Some items have two answers.

1. We only have a few ___tea bags___ left.
2. Do we have any more _____ ?
3. There's just a little _____ left.
4. We don't have many _____ left.
5. We have a lot of _____ left.

Ways to say it

1 APOLOGIZE FOR BEING LATE

● I'm sorry I'm late. *I got caught in traffic.*
○ Oh, that's O.K.

○ I had time to *clean up* before you came. | □ I just got here myself. I've only been here for *a little while.*

Some reasons for being late
I got caught in traffic. I couldn't find a parking space. My car wouldn't start. I missed my bus. I overslept.

2 STATE A CONCLUSION

End the conversation with an appropriate suggestion or offer.

● *I've been sneezing all day.*
○ You must *be getting a cold.* Why don't you go lie down? I'll bring you some aspirin.

Some facts	Some conclusions
I've been sneezing all day. I have a terrible toothache. I haven't sat down all day. I haven't eaten all day.	You have a cavity. You're getting a cold. You're starving (very hungry). You're exhausted.

sit   sat   sat

You probably have a cold. = You must have a cold.
You're probably getting a cold. = You must be getting a cold.

3 FIGURE OUT WHERE YOU LEFT SOMETHING

● Now, what did I do with my *car keys?*
○ *They* | may / might | be *in your coat pocket.*

Some misplaced objects	Some places to look
car keys house keys glasses watch appointment book	coat pocket, car coat pocket, door desk, kitchen table bedroom, bathroom briefcase, work

● Good idea. I'll check there. | ● I just looked there.
○ Well, then maybe you left *them in the car.*

4 TALK ABOUT QUANTITY

● Do we have any *toothpaste?*
○ (We may be out of *it.*) Look *in the medicine cabinet.*

● Oh, here *it is.* I found *it.* | ● There | 's only a *little* / 's *not much* | left. | ● I've already looked there.
○ We must not have any more then.

Some things to look for	
toothpaste	soap
shampoo	toilet paper
Scotch tape	paper clips
Band-Aids	detergent

Some places to look
in the medicine cabinet under the kitchen sink in the bathroom closet in the desk drawer

Count nouns	Mass nouns
There are only a few left. There aren't many left.	There's only a little left. There's not much left.

5   *MAY, MIGHT,* AND *MUST*

Affirmative statements

He	may might	have	a headache.
		stay	home tomorrow.
		be getting	sick.

| He | must | have | the flu. |
| | | be working | too hard. |

> *May* and *might* express possibility, whereas *must* expresses a logical conclusion. Compare:
>
> | Fact: All the lights are off at John's house. | Possibilities: He may be asleep. He might be out. |
> | Fact: His car isn't there, either. | Conclusion: He must be out. |

Negative statements

He	may might	not	have	any aspirin.
			come	to work tomorrow.
			be eating	the right food.

| He | must | not | have | a cold. |
| | | | be getting | enough sleep. |

> *May* and *might* can also be used to talk about possibilities in the future:
>
> I might go to the beach this weekend.
> I may not take a vacation this summer.

> Like *can* and *should,* the modal auxiliaries *may, might,* and *must* have the same form for all pronouns and are followed by the base form of the verb. Compare the formation of sentences in the present and present continuous tenses:
>
> He *has* a headache. ▶ He may *have* a headache.
> He*'s getting* the flu. ▶ He may *be getting* the flu.

6   Complete the conversations using *may, might,* or *must* in your answers.

1. ● I can't understand where Paul is.
   ○ <u>*He might be at work*</u> . I'll call his office.

2. ● Is Ellen Fox there?
   ○ Ellen Fox? _____ .
   ● Oh, I'm sorry.

3. ● I'll see you at the theater.
   ○ _____ . It depends on how much work I have.

4. ● I haven't eaten all day.
   ○ _____ .
   ● No, actually, I'm not hungry at all. I have a terrible headache.
   ○ _____ .

5. ● I've been exhausted all week.
   ○ _____ .
   ● That's very possible. I never get to sleep before midnight.

7   (MAKE A REQUEST)

First request the items in the box. Then ask for things you really need.

● I'm going to the *grocery store.* Is there anything you need?
○ Could you get me *a roll of paper towels?* I just *ran out of them.*
● Sure. Any special kind?
○ Yes. *Round-up.*   ○ No, any kind.

| I don't care. It doesn't matter. |

You need . . .	You just . . .
a roll of (*Round-up*) paper towels.	used it up. ran out of them.
a bottle of shampoo. some apples.	ate the last one. ran out of it.
a tube of (*Smile*) toothpaste.	used the last one.
a box of (*All-Bright*) detergent.	

> Ways you've said it
>
> Could you get me . . . ?

ASK WHERE SOMETHING IS

Using the floor plan, match each item with its location. Then practice the conversation.

● Could you tell me where the *carrots are*?
○ *They're behind the lettuce.*

Some items	Some locations
carrots	in the front of the store
chicken	in the back of the store
tissues	against the wall
bread	(up) on top
napkins	(down) on the bottom
	above the toilet paper
	below the toilet paper
	behind the lettuce

Ways you've said it

next to
across from
in front/back of
on the right/left

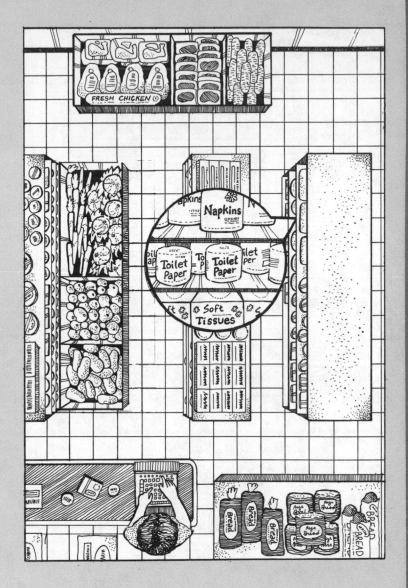

 MAKE DINNER

Act out the conversation. Play Role A or Role B.

Role A

You're visiting your sister, and you both want to cook something interesting for dinner. Follow these steps:

1. Decide what to make.
2. Find out what food your sister has and what you'll need to buy.
3. Offer to go to the store. Find out if she needs anything else before you go.

Role B

Your brother is visiting you, and you've both decided to make something good for dinner. Follow these steps:

1. Decide what to make.
2. Figure out what food you have and what you'll need to buy. Use expressions such as *a little left*. If you're not sure if you have something, tell your brother where to look. (*It might be up on top . . .*)

Start like this:
● *What do you want to have for dinner?*
○ *Why don't we make . . . ?*

I'm afraid we don't have many left.

Doug is shopping for a clock radio.

1

Clerk: Is there anything I can help you with or are you just looking?

Doug: I'm looking for a clock radio. Are these the only ones you have?

Clerk: Yes, I'm afraid we don't have many left. Did you have a particular one in mind?

Doug: No, not really. I was just trying to get an idea of what there was.

Clerk: This one is very nice. It has an AM/FM radio, a lighted dial . . .

Doug: Does it come in another color?

Clerk: It did come in white, but I don't see any, so we must have sold the last one. The red's quite attractive, though. Is it a gift or for yourself?

Doug: It's for myself. What about that one way up on top?

Clerk: That one's a little more expensive. Would you like me to get it down for you?

Doug: Please. . . . Do you mind if I try it?

Clerk: No, not at all. (*Doug turns on radio*)

Voice: Good afternoon and welcome to "A Little Afternoon Music." I'm your host, Laura Enders. We've got lots of wonderful . . .

Doug: Laura Enders!

Clerk: I beg your pardon?

Doug: Uh . . . nothing. I guess I'll take it.

Clerk: If you could step over here, please. . . .

2. Figure it out

Say *Right*, *Wrong*, or *I don't know.*

1. The radio is a Christmas present for Doug's father. *Wrong.*
2. The store doesn't have many clock radios left.
3. Doug buys the more expensive radio.
4. Laura Enders has her own radio show.
5. Doug needs a clock radio because he often oversleeps.

3. Listen in

Doug is listening to the weather report on his new radio. Read the statements below. Then listen to the report and choose *a* or *b*.

1. Sunday's temperature is going to be _____ .
   a. 10° (degrees)
   b. −10°

2. It's going to be _____ .
   a. sunny
   b. cloudy

111

Your turn

Ellen Jones didn't come to work today. Why not? What happened yesterday?

1.

2.

3.

4.

Now play the role of one of the people in each picture, and, with a partner, act out a conversation for each one.

Say it right

Say the phrases below. Then practice the conversation. 📼

cár keys   cóat pocket   hóuse keys   tóilet paper   páper clips   tóothpaste

- Where are your car keys?
○ They're in my coat pocket—with my house keys.
- Let's see. . . . We need toilet paper, paper clips, and toothpaste. Anything else?
○ No, that's it.

112

On your own

Read the advice column. Then answer these questions.

1. How many people have colds right now?
   One out of every eight.
2. How do most people catch colds?
3. What advice do doctors give about vitamin C?
4. What are three things you should do when you have a cold?
5. How can you protect other people when you have a cold?

MEDICAL ADVICE
By Dr. Elaine Ramsey

DEAR DR. RAMSEY:
I seem to get colds all the time. Is there anything I can do to prevent them? What should I do after I've caught one?
—FRUSTRATED

DEAR FRUSTRATED:
The common cold is the most frequent of all illnesses. At any given moment, about one out of every eight people has one. Most people get colds by touching things that a person with a cold has used. You can even catch a cold by shaking hands. So if someone you know has a cold, you should not use the same cups, glasses, dishes, or telephone.

Although there is no permanent cure for the cold, doctors believe that vitamins can help prevent one. Many doctors recommend vitamin C to prevent colds, and some doctors suggest that you take large amounts when you begin to get sick. Yet it is not really known whether vitamin C is truly helpful.

The body needs healthy food to fight a cold. If you have a cold, you should eat well, but not overeat, and you should drink lots of liquids, especially juices. Also be sure to get enough rest and stay warm. If your body aches, you can take one to two aspirin every four hours. Some research shows, however, that taking aspirin can make your cold last longer.

When you have a cold, you should also try to protect other people. Cover your mouth and nose when you cough or sneeze. Put all your used tissues in a paper bag, and throw away the bag yourself so that no one else will have to touch it. Wash all objects that you touch with very hot water before anyone else uses them.

Words

See p. 108 for a list of household items and p. 110 for a list of prepositions.

get caught in	toothache	closet	bottle	wouldn't (would)	myself
run out of	cavity	sink (n)	tube	sneeze (v)	exhausted
I don't care.	appointment book	wall	box	must	a little while
It doesn't matter.	medicine cabinet	coat	miss (a bus)	sat (sit)	a little/not much left
parking space	desk drawer	watch (n)	oversleep	starve	

15. Catching up

Graduation day, 1977

Try this

Look at the picture. Then choose a partner and discuss these questions:

1. What were you doing five years ago? Ten years ago? What have you done since then? What are you doing now?
2. Has your life changed much in the last five (or ten) years? How?
3. Have you changed much in the last five (or ten) years? How?

Two old college friends from the University of Michigan, Betsy Dodd and David Miller, run into each other in Barcelona.

A
- ● Betsy
- ○ David

- ● David Miller?
- ○ Betsy Dodd! In Barcelona! I don't believe it! Hey, you haven't changed a bit!
- ● Neither have you!
- ○ Oh, come on now, I used to have more hair, didn't I?
- ● Well, now that you mention it . . .
- ○ So, how have you been? What brings you to Barcelona?
- ● I'm here on vacation. You too?
- ○ Do I *still* look like a tourist? I live here.
- ● You're kidding! How long have you been living here?
- ○ For three years.
- ● Great! What do you do here?
- ○ Well, I'm studying Catalan and I've been teaching English since the fall. How about you?
- ● I'm an architect.
- ○ Hey, not bad.
- ● And you're not going to believe this—I'm still living in Ann Arbor.
- ○ No kidding!
- ● My husband's on the faculty at the U. of M.
- ○ Oh, so you're married. Any children?
- ● Not yet.
- ○ Is your husband here?
- ● Well, not right here. He's back at the hotel resting.

114

○ Gee, I haven't been back to Ann Arbor in years . . . not since we graduated. Has it changed much?

● Oh, not that much. You'd still recognize it! You know, it's great seeing you again. I've really lost touch with everyone from back then.

○ So have I. Let's keep in touch . . . .

● Listen, why don't we go get coffee somewhere?

○ Oh, I'd like to, but I've really got to get going. I teach at four. But how about dinner? You and your husband can meet me where I teach.

● Sounds great!

○ Here's the address. It's right near Plaza Molina. I finish at ten.

● Ten? For dinner?

○ Hey, this is Spain, remember?

Figure it out

1. Say *Right*, *Wrong*, or *I don't know*.

1. Betsy and David haven't seen each other recently.   *Right.*
2. Betsy has been to Spain before.
3. Betsy and David were friends in Ann Arbor.
4. Betsy's husband teaches at the University of Michigan.
5. Betsy's husband must be tired.
6. David still writes to a few of the people he and Betsy knew.

2. Fill in the blanks with *no*, *not*, or *neither*.

1. _*Neither*_ have I.
2. _____ yet.
3. _____ kidding!
4. _____ since we graduated.

3. Find another way to say it.

1. Why are you in Barcelona?
   What brings you to Barcelona?
2. How long have you lived here?
3. from those days
4. I have to go.

Ways to say it

1 GREET SOMEONE AFTER A LONG TIME

These people all graduated from the University of Michigan in 1977. How have they changed? Some have changed a lot more than others. Match.

Robert Barnes

Jim Jacobs

Robert	let her hair grow.
Jim	used to have more hair.
Andrea	shaved off his beard.
Salma	has lost a lot of weight.
	wears contact lenses now.
	used to be a little thinner.

Andrea London

Salma Rahal

Now imagine that you were also a student at the University of Michigan, and you knew all these people. One of them runs into you and greets you warmly.

● *Carmen Garcia*!

○ *Robert Barnes*! ○ *Jim Jacobs*!

○ I haven't seen you in so long! How have you been?
● *Fine.* How about you?
○ *Not bad.*

○ You know, you haven't changed a bit, *Robert*!
● Oh, come on. *I used to have more hair.*

○ I didn't recognize you at first, *Jim*. You've really changed!
● Well, *I've lost a lot of weight.*

2 TALK ABOUT PEOPLE YOU KNEW

Continue the conversation you started in exercise 1. Play the role of Carmen and talk to one of the people in the pictures.

Some ways to keep in touch

get together (with someone)   call someone up
write (to someone)   talk (to someone)
hear from someone   see someone

write   wrote   written

● Do you still keep in touch with anyone from school?

○ Yes. I still *get together with Salma from time to time.*
● (Oh, so do I.)

○ Well, *Jim* and I used to *write (to each other) occasionally,* but I haven't *heard from him in over a year.*

○ No. I've really lost touch with everyone.
● (So have I.)

◄ In present perfect negative statements, either *in* or *for* is used before a period of time.

3 | CATCH UP ON WHAT SOMEONE HAS DONE

● Have you *been (back) to Ann Arbor* recently?

○ Yes. *I've been back twice.*   ○ No, not *in a long time.*
                                  ● (Neither have I.)

Have you . . .?	Not . . .	
been back to Ann Arbor heard from Salma gone anywhere interesting done anything exciting read any good books	in	a long time. a while.
	since	last year. we graduated.

4 | Close-up

SHORT NEGATIVE STATEMENTS
WITHOUT VERBS

Do you have any children?	We don't have any yet. Not yet.
Have you been to Chicago?	I haven't been there since 1980. Not since 1980.
Are you still teaching French?	I'm not teaching anymore. Not anymore.

5 | Complete each conversation with an appropriate short negative statement.

1. ● Have you finished *Eye of the Needle?*
   ○ ___*Not yet*___ . I still have twenty-five pages to go.

2. ● Do you ever see Mary?
   ○ _____ . Maybe once or twice a year.

3. ● You're a student at Ohio State, aren't you?
   ○ _____ . I graduated in June.

4. ● Have you seen Bruce recently?
   ○ _____ last summer.

5. ● Could you help me for a minute?
   ○ _____ . I'm late for class.

6. ● Have you been skiing recently?
   ○ No, _____ . It's been at least three years.

6 | TALK ABOUT DURATION

● How long have you | lived / been living | in *Chicago?*

○ (I've been living here) *since last fall.*
● How long have you been studying English?
○ *For a couple of years.*
● Oh, you speak really well.

PRESENT PERFECT CONTINUOUS

Information questions

How long	have	you they	been	working teaching	here?
	has	he she			

Affirmative statements

I We They	've	been	working teaching	here	for nine years. since 1976.
He She	's				

> When the verbs *live, work, study,* and *teach* are used with expressions of duration, there is little difference in meaning between the present perfect and the present perfect continuous.

8 **Read about Frank Lynch and Martha and John Corning. Then ask questions about them using *How long . . . ?* and the present perfect continuous of these verbs: *work, live, teach,* and *study.* Another student will answer your questions.**

● *How long has Frank Lynch been working at Acme Plumbing?*
○ *He's been working there . . .*

Frank Lynch is a plumber at Acme Plumbing. He started working there when he first moved to Akron, Ohio. He was twenty then. He's sixty now.

Martha and John Corning moved to Washington, D.C. two years ago. Martha teaches first grade. She started teaching six years ago. She'd like to teach deaf children, so last fall she started studying American Sign Language. John got his present job for the government two years ago.

9 MAKE SUGGESTIONS

● Why don't we *go get coffee* somewhere?

○ ACCEPT AND SUGGEST A PLACE.

○ But let's keep in touch. Here's my phone number. . . .

○ I'd like to, but I've really got to get going. *I'm supposed to be somewhere in five minutes.*

○ But let's get together another time. MAKE A SUGGESTION.

Some reasons for refusing
I'm supposed to be somewhere in five minutes.
I've got a class in a little while.
I've got to run a lot of errands .
I've got to do a million things.
I've got to get to the bank before it closes.

Here we are again.

Laura and Terry are flying home to Columbus for the holidays. 🔲

1. Listen in 🔲

Laura has just arrived at the airport, where Terry is waiting for her. Read the statements below. Then listen to the conversation and say *Right* or *Wrong*.

1. Terry has been waiting for Laura for a long time.
2. Laura hasn't eaten, but Terry has.
3. Laura isn't going to buy something to eat at the snack bar.

2

Laura: Well, I got a letter from Chuck today.
Terry: Oh, what did he have to say?
Laura: Well, all in all, he seems pretty happy. He likes Portland, and he's meeting some really nice people.
Terry: Does he still want you to go out there?
Laura: He says he does.
Terry: And how are *you* feeling?
Laura: Sad. I miss him. But I think I've made the right decision, at least for now.
Terry: (*Noticing Doug*) I don't believe it! Here comes the guy who lives downstairs from me.
Doug: If it isn't the Enders sisters! Well, here we are again, Laura!
Terry: Hey, wait a minute. . . . Do you two know each other?
Laura: You *do* look awfully familiar. *Have* we met somewhere?
Doug: On my first plane ride from Columbus to Chicago. Doug Lee . . . I was coming here for a job interview. You were reading *Eye of the Needle.* . . .
Laura: Oh, right! You've got a good memory.
Doug: So, how did you like it?
Laura: What?
Doug: *Eye of the Needle.*
Laura: Great ending!
Doug: Yeah, I thought so, too. Oh, and you'll be happy to hear, I got the job.
Laura: Congratulations! What kind of job is it? . . .

3. Figure it out

Say *Right*, *Wrong*, or *I don't know.*

1. Chuck moved to Portland.   *Right.*
2. Laura has decided to stay in Chicago.
3. Laura doesn't think about Chuck anymore.
4. Laura doesn't recognize Doug at first.
5. Terry and Doug planned to take the same plane.
6. Doug hasn't seen his family since he moved to Chicago.

Your turn

Ana and Carlos Ortega got married in the summer of 1973, right after they finished college. How have their lives changed since then? Discuss this question in groups.

Spring, 1973

Fall, 1983

How have you changed in the past ten years? What about your appearance? What about your interests? What about your personality? How do you think you will change in the next ten years? Discuss these questions in groups.

Say it right

Say the words below. Then practice the conversations. 🔲

eaten [íytṇ]   written [rítṇ]   gotten [gátṇ]

1. ● I haven't gotten a letter from Mark in six months.
   ○ Neither have I, and I've written to him twice. I hope he's O.K.

2. ● Have you eaten at Ferdinand's Steak House recently?
   ○ No, I haven't eaten there since last summer.

On your own

Dear Editor:

What is happening to English? It's almost painful to hear how people speak these days. They use "who" when they should use "whom," the past tense when they should use the present perfect, and adjectives when they should use adverbs. What has happened to the grammar rules I learned when I was a boy? I realize that was many years ago, and I've learned that many things in life change, but correct grammar shouldn't be one of them.

Have the schools simply stopped teaching grammar? Certainly many educated people don't sound like they have ever studied it. If we don't do something to solve this problem soon, there won't be anyone left who knows what the correct rules are.

THOMAS PERKINS
Plainfield

Dear Editor:

As an English teacher, I must disagree with Thomas Perkins, whose letter appeared in your newspaper on June 28. He complains that people no longer speak correctly and that the schools should do something to solve this problem. Naturally, teachers are aware that grammar is important, but languages are always changing. If Mr. Perkins doesn't believe this, he should look at the language of Shakespeare's time. Much of it sounds strange to us, and some of it is very hard to understand. Yet I'm sure that even Mr. Perkins would agree that Shakespeare's English was correct.

If Mr. Perkins thinks that it is unfair to go back almost four hundred years, he should look at the 1918 grammar text, *Outline of English Grammar*, by J. C. Nesfield. He will find words such as "hither," "thither," and "whither," which have all been replaced by "here," "there," and "where." The present perfect has also changed. Fifty years ago it was correct to say "hast." In fact, according to those rules, Mr. Perkins should have written, "What hast happened to the grammar rules I learned when I was a boy?" It is important to remember that while we are teaching the rules, they are in the process of changing.

CYNTHIA HAWTHORNE
Middletown

Read the letters to the editor of *Plainfield News*. Then match each pronoun in italics with the word or phrase it refers to.

1. *They* use "who" when they should use "whom." ————
2. I realize *that* was many years ago.
3. Many educated people don't sound like they have ever studied *it*.
4. *He* complains that people no longer speak correctly.
5. If Mr. Perkins doesn't believe *this,* he should look at the language of Shakespeare's time.
6. Some of *it* is very hard to understand.

a. Mr. Perkins
b. people
c. Languages are always changing.
d. Shakespeare's English
e. when I was a boy
f. grammar

Words

contact lenses	let one's hair grow	call up	deaf
plumber	lose touch	shave off	a bit
government	keep in touch	get going	written (write)
recognize	hear from	thin	

16. Review

It must be your brother.

Sam and Joan Weber get an early morning phone call. 📼

Joan: *(Rrring, rrring)* Will you get it, Sam? It must be your brother. He's the only one who calls this early.
Sam: Hello?
Fred: Hello, Sammy. I hope I'm not disturbing you.
Sam: Uh, no, I was just sleeping. *(Yawns)*
Fred: Oh, I'm sorry I woke you up. Do you want me to call back later?
Sam: No, no, that's O.K., Fred. Just let me try to open my left eye.
Fred: I always forget you like to sleep late on Saturday mornings.
Sam: Late? It's seven o'clock!
Fred: It's the nicest time of the day.
Sam: Funny, I've always liked ten o'clock better.
Fred: Well, I won't keep you. I just wanted to tell you that Aunt Thelma and Uncle Max are coming here tomorrow from St. Louis to visit Mom and Dad. They're on their way to a dentists' convention in Chicago.
Sam: Oh, yeah? *(Yawns)*
Fred: Joyce and I are having everyone over for dinner tomorrow night. Do you and Joan think you can make it?
Sam: Well, I don't think we're doing anything, but I'll have to check with Joan.
Fred: Oh, isn't she there?
Sam: Well, I know you might find this hard to believe, but Joan's still asleep.
Fred: Oh, well, I hope you can come. Joyce is making her special chicken.
Sam: Well, I'll call you later and let you know.
Fred: O.K. Bye, Sammy.
Sam: Bye, Fred.

A few hours later, Sam tells Joan about the phone call. Combine each pair of sentences in brackets into one sentence. Then complete Sam's part of the conversation, using the information from the previous conversation.

Joan: [What did your brother want? You haven't told me.] *You haven't told me what your brother wanted.*
Sam: _____ .
Joan: [Which ones are Thelma and Max? I can never remember.]
Sam: _____ .
Joan: Oh, that's right. The ones with the big dogs. [What are they making for dinner? Did he say?]
Sam: _____ .
Joan: Just as I thought. Well, we're not doing anything tomorrow evening. [What time do they want us to be there? Find out.]
Sam: _____ .

2 **What happened to Thelma and Max? Read the statements below. Then listen to the conversation and choose *a*, *b*, or *c*.**

1. Thelma and Max are late because _____ .
   a. they left late
   b. they got caught in traffic
   c. they had an accident

2. Thelma says they'll be there _____ .
   a. by four
   b. around a quarter after four
   c. by five

3 **Everyone has a compliment for Joyce. Fill in each blank with the correct form of one of these verbs: *taste*, *smell*, *sound*, or *look*.**

Thelma: Oh, your table <u>*looks*</u> so nice.
Max: And something _____ wonderful.
Sam: It must be Joyce's famous chicken.
Joyce: You're right: I make it with peppers and lots of garlic.
Joan: It _____ delicious.

Fred: Well, let me serve all of you before it gets cold.
Joyce: *(A few minutes later)* So, how does it _____ ?
Sam's mother: Wonderful, Joyce. You've done it again.
Sam's father: Joyce's chicken always _____ wonderful.

4 **Act out the conversation. One student will play the role of Fred Weber. The other will play the role of one of his guests.**

Fred:

1. Offer your guest food. You're serving chicken, string beans, French fries, and salad. Use these expressions:

Help yourself.
Would you care for any . . . ?

2. After your guest has finished eating, offer him or her more food. Use these expressions:

a lot (left)	still some (left)
a little (left)	a few (left)
some more	another
something else	

   Then offer your guest coffee or tea.

Guest:

Respond to Fred Weber. Here are some expressions you may use:

a little	some	a few
some more	another	

I'm interested in the job you advertised.

1 Lisa Parish is calling about a job that was advertised in the paper. A receptionist connects her to Mrs. Thompson. Combine each pair of sentences in brackets into one sentence.

● Rhoda Thompson speaking.

○ Hello, Mrs. Thompson, my name is Lisa Parish. [I'm interested in the job. You advertised the job in Sunday's paper.] *I'm interested in the job (that) you advertised in Sunday's paper.*

● Oh, yes, the receptionist's job. [Well, Ms. Parish, we're looking for someone. The person should have some experience.] Have you worked as a receptionist before?

○ [Yes, I used to work for a company. The company sold photo albums.] [I answered the phone and greeted people. People came into the office.]

● Oh, well, that sounds good. Could you come in for an interview tomorrow afternoon at two?

○ Yes. You're on Division Street, aren't you?

● Yes, at 256. [It's the tall building. The building is on the corner of Division and Ludlow.] [Do you have a letter of reference from the company? You used to work for the company.]

○ Yes, I do. I'll bring it with me tomorrow.

2 Complete the letter. Fill in each blank with one of the two words given.

3829 Honeybrook Avenue
Dayton, Ohio 45415
April 12, 1984

Office of Field Services
Division of Personnel
65 Court Street, Lobby Level
Brooklyn, NY 11201

Dear Sir/Madam:

I'm writing concerning the job of bilingual school psychologist which you advertised in last Sunday's <u>New York Times</u>. My husband and I are planning to move to the New York area this summer, and I'm very _____ in finding employment for the fall. I've worked as a school psychologist in the Dayton school system _____ the last five years. I speak Spanish very _____ with native fluency. I enjoy _____ with both elementary and high school students, and I'm very _____ at the possibility of finding similar work in New York.

I'm planning to be in New York in June, but I can come for an interview _____ if you wish. Enclosed is my résumé.

Sincerely yours,

Barbara Menéndez
...ndez

interested/interesting

for/since
good/well
working/to work
excited/exciting

early/earlier

3 Read the three ads below. Then listen to three conversations about them and match each conversation with the correct ad. 🔲

1 ____ a
2 ____ b
3 ____ c

ⓐ
PHYSICAL THERAPIST
Immediate opening for an experienced or recent graduate physical therapist. Opportunity to work in a modern physical therapy department. 22 vacation days, excellent benefits. Send résumé to:

Margaret Fair
Chief Physical Therapist
Whitman Hospital
983 Troy Avenue
Mobile, Alabama 36610

ⓑ
SOCIAL WORKER
Excellent opportunity in private agency serving mainly elderly clients. Car needed for home visits. Master of Social Work preferred. Salary $15–20,000 depending on experience. Send résumé to:

Leslie Joseph, Director
Senior Services Agency
65 Wendell Street
Cambridge, Massachusetts 02138

ⓒ
STAFF ACCOUNTANT
Immediate opening for an accountant with experience in the hospital field. Degree preferred.
Salary $19,000 + . Please send résumé to:

Mr. L. Vincent
Employment Coordinator
Salk Hospital
3100 N.W. 88th Avenue
Coral Springs, Fla. 33065

4 These three people have all applied for the position described in the ad on the right. Read the ad and the qualifications of the three candidates. Then compare the candidates, and finally, decide which one is best for the job. Here are some new words you can use: *qualified, experienced, responsible,* and *mature.*

RECEPTIONIST/SECRETARY — Capable and reliable individual to work in local sales office of international firm. Requires person with excellent typing and office skills and good interpersonal skills. Must have a pleasant telephone voice. Previous sales office experience preferred, but not essential. Position offers excellent salary and benefits. Call 396-7200 between 9 and 5 weekdays.

Darlene Rodgers is 24 years old. She has worked as a secretary in a sales office for the past three years. She types 75 words a minute. She speaks a little Spanish. She's quiet, but very pleasant and easy to get along with.

Barbara Murphy is 40 years old. She had ten years' experience as a secretary. She stopped working eight years ago to have children. She types 70 words a minute. She's very pleasant and cheerful and enjoys working with people.

Glen Williams is 24 years old. He has done some part-time secretarial work for the past six months and is now looking for a full-time job. He types 85 words a minute. He speaks German and French fluently. He hasn't done sales work. He's friendly and outgoing.

Glen Williams types faster than either Darlene Rogers or Barbara Murphy, but Darlene Rogers . . .

We're thinking of going to Thailand.

 Carol Cole runs into her friend Amy and has this conversation. For each set of brackets, combine the unfinished sentence with the question that follows it.

Carol: Barry and I are thinking of going to Thailand for our vacation this year.

Amy: That sounds exciting! During the summer?

Carol: Sometime during the summer. [We're not sure yet . . . When are we going?] [It depends on . . . When can we both take a month off from work?] *We're not sure yet when we're going. . . .*

Amy: [Do you know . . . ? Who used to live in Thailand?] My brother.

Carol: No kidding! [I'd love to ask him . . . Where should we go and what should we see?]

Amy: Well, he's coming to visit sometime next month. Why don't we all get together then?

Carol: I'd really like that. [Do you happen to know . . . ? What's the weather like in Thailand?]

Amy: I think it's pretty hot and humid most of the year. And there's a rainy season. [But I'm not sure . . . When is it?] [It might depend on . . . What part of the country are you going to?]

Carol: [Well, let me know . . . When is your brother coming here?]

Amy: I will, as soon as I find out.

2

The Coles are getting ready for their trip. Offer to help them with each of the items below. Start each sentence with *if.*

1. They might not have a camera.
   If you don't have a camera . . .

2. They might need a ride to the airport.

3. They might want someone to pick up their mail.

4. They might need someone to water their plants.

3 Barry and Carol want to make sure they haven't forgotten anything. Barry is looking at their "Things to do" list and asking Carol questions. Match the two parts of each sentence.

1. Our plane leaves at 8:05,
2. You have our passports,
3. You've called your parents to say good-bye,
4. You bought some shampoo,
5. Tom is picking us up at 6:30,
6. Tom knows what time the plane leaves,
7. Sue's going to water the plants,
8. Sue's picked up our key,
9. Sue has your parents' phone number,
10. You're carrying the traveler's checks in your purse,

a. didn't you?
b. hasn't she?
c. aren't you?
d. don't you?
e. isn't she?
f. doesn't it?
g. isn't he?
h. doesn't he?
i. haven't you?
j. doesn't she?

4 When they get to the airport, Barry can't seem to find the tickets. Complete Carol's part of the conversation by suggesting where the tickets might be. Use *may, might,* or *must* in your answers.

Barry: Now what did I do with the tickets?
Carol: _____ .
Barry: I just looked there.
Carol: _____ .
Barry: I've already looked there, too. I hope I didn't leave them at home.
Carol: Now I remember! They were on the kitchen table, and I picked them up. _____ .

5 Using the map and the clues below, match these seven Thai cities with their locations.

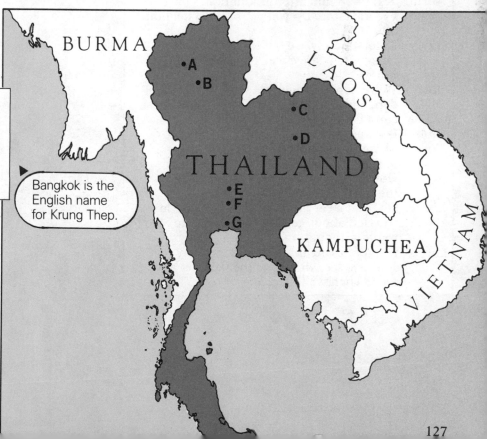

1. Ayutthaya	[ayúwtʰayá]	a
2. Bangkok		b
3. Chiengmai	[čéŋmay]	c
4. Khon Kaen	[kʰón kén]	d
5. Lampang	[lampáŋ]	e
6. Lop Buri	[lówp borí]	f
7. Udon Thani	[udón tʰaní]	g

Bangkok is the English name for Krung Thep.

Clues:

1. Khon Kaen is northeast of Lop Buri.
2. Khon Kaen is directly south of Udon Thani.
3. Ayutthaya is about halfway between Lop Buri and Bangkok.
4. Chiengmai is the farthest one from Bangkok.
5. Lampang is closer to Lop Buri than it is to Bangkok.

127

Reunion

The class of 1963 of Colonel White High School in Dayton, Ohio, is having its twentieth reunion. 📼

Norm: Larry Quinn! How have you been?

Larry: Norm Lewis! It's good to see you again. You haven't changed at all, you know, except your hair's a little longer.

Norm: Well, you don't look much different, but you sure sound different.

Larry: That's because I spent ten years in London. I suppose I've picked up a bit of an accent. And I also married an Englishwoman and have two children with British accents. By the way, this is my wife, Libby. Norm Lewis.

Norm: Nice to meet you, Libby.

Libby: How do you do, Norm.

Norm: So, you're living in the States now?

Larry: Yes, we moved to New York two years ago.

Norm: That really sounds great, living in England. I lived in Germany until I was two—my father was in the army—but that's the last time I was out of the U.S. Maybe someday I'll save enough money, and Julie and I will go to Europe. Julie's my wife.

Larry: Oh, so you got married, did you?

Norm: Yes, two years after graduation. I have five kids, too. Do you get back to London often?

Libby: Unfortunately, we haven't managed to make a trip since we've been in the States.

Larry: We're hoping to go this year, but it depends on our jobs. We're not sure we can take time off.

Libby: Is your wife here, Norm?

Norm: She just left. She doesn't really like big parties. I'd really like you to meet her. How about coming over tonight after the party or tomorrow?

Libby: Oh, that's very kind of you. I'm a little worried about getting home too late tonight, though.

Larry: Yes, tomorrow might be better. Why don't we see what time the party is over? Then we'll decide.

📘 **Complete each of these statements with a time expression. Use the information in the conversation.**

1. Larry and Libby have lived in New York
   _____ .

2. Larry and Libby haven't been back to London
   _____ .

3. Norm and Julie have been married
   _____ .

4. Norm has lived in the U.S.
   _____ .

2 **Larry, Libby, and Norm are all talking about tentative plans they have. What are they? Write three sentences beginning with *if*.**

If Norm and Julie save enough money . . .

COLONEL WHITE HIGH SCHOOL
CLASS of 1963

128

3 These are parts of some of the other conversations taking place at the reunion. Fill in each blank with the correct form of one of the expressions in the box below. Include the prepositions after the two-word verbs where necessary.

be back (from)	get along (with)	get together (with)	hear of	move in (to)
come over (to)	get back (from)	hear from	know of	run out (of)

1. ● So you're thinking of moving back to Dayton?
   ○ Yes, I'd like to find a job in computers.
   ● Well, I don't _know of_ anything, but if I _____ something, I'll let you know.

2. ● Do you ever see Vicki Bernie?
   ○ We used to write, but I haven't _____ her in a long time.

3. ● It's so great seeing you again.
   ○ Yes, we really ought to _____ more often.
   ● Well, how about _____ next weekend?

4. ● When did you _____ France?
   ○ Let's see now, we've _____ for about six months now.

4 Look at Brad Miller, Marta Miller, and Jim Harper on the right. Then complete this conversation. There is more than one way to complete it.

● I was just talking to Brad Miller.
○ Which one is he?
● He's the one _____ .
   He introduced me to his wife.
   She seems interesting
   She's the one _____ .
○ Who's the tall man _____ ?
● Oh, that's Jim, uh . . . what's his last name again? . Harper, that's it. Jim Harper. He used to be on the basketball team.

5 Two women are talking about someone at the reunion. Look at Jack, Henry, and Bill in the picture. Then listen to the conversation and choose a, b, or c. ▭

The women are talking about _____ .
a. Jack   b. Henry   c. Bill

Words

The word list contains the 500 productive words included in the textbook, as well as all receptive words introduced. Productive words are those that students should know how to use. Receptive words are those that students need only understand. The letter R appears next to each receptive word. For each productive word, the page number refers to the place where it was first introduced productively. Much of the productive vocabulary, however, is introduced receptively in earlier units. The word list does not include the following lexical sets: irregular verbs, parts of a house, and weights and measures. For these, refer to the appendix on pp. 134–135. For the seasons in the Northern Hemisphere, see p. 12; for indefinite compounds, see p. 36; for comparative and superlative forms of adjectives, see pp. 36–37; for sports, see pp. 52–53; for compass directions, see p. 77; for abbreviations, see p. 82; and for soup ingredients, see p. 104.

a bit 116
a block away 84
above 110
accent 28
accurate R 97
ache (v) R 113
a couple of 21
actually 45
a day 52
adolescent R 15
adventure R 26
advertise 84
advertising
  agency 4
a few of 21
afford R 87
against 110
airline (adj) R 57
alike 54
a little while 108
alive R 18
all in all R 119
all moved in R 87
all one's life 12
all red 102
almond R 98
a long time 12
American Sign
  Language R 118
AM/FM R 111
another 100
anxious R 31
any good 20
any kind 109
anymore 11
Any special
  kind? 109
Anything exciting
  going on? R 18
appearance R 120
apply for R 47
appointment
  book 108
archeological R 81
archeology R 66
area R 34
Are you free? R 19
around here R 50
arrive 90

as a matter of
  fact 5
as if R 103
as if you were
  (walking) R 57
asleep R 122
assistant R 17
Atchoo! R 106
athletics R 15
Atlantic R 30
at least 117
atmosphere 36
attractions R 80
awake 68
a little while 108

baby-sit R 31
baby-sitter 93
back at (the
  hotel) R 114
backpack 53
back then R 115
backward R 49
badly 28
bake 45
balanced
  (adj) R 49
bare R 87
barometer R 97
bath R 82
bathroom
  (adj) R 39
be a lot like
  (someone) 54
bean 28
be awake 68
Bedouins R 89
beginning (n) R 10
behind 110
be in (the office) 46
below 110
bending (n) R 57
bent (bend) R 57
be out R 47
best 28
be supposed to 44
Be sure and
  come. R 71
bicycle shop 53

bike (bicycle) 53
Bless you. R 106
blood
  circulation R 57
borrow 44
both 4
both of 14
bottle 109
branch (n) R 58
bridge R 33
broiled R 98
broken
  English R 30
brought (bring)
  over R 26
by (a certain
  time) 46
by any
  chance R 39

calculate R 56
calendar 68
call up 116
camper R 15
campgrounds R 74
canyon R 74
captain R 16
care for 76
carefully 31
carpenter 59
carry (have) R 39
carry (hold) R 39
cash R 39
casual R 34
catch a cold R 113
catch (a plane) R 2
catch up on 92
cause (n) R 96
cavity 108
census R 26
central 77
centrally 85
ceremony 22
chance R 15
change (v–
  intrans) 116
change planes 90
chapter 77
character R 41

check (n) 100
check (v) 68
cheerful 125
chemistry R 16
chocolate cake 45
cigar R 99
clearly 94
client R 71
cliff dwelling 78
clock radio R 111
closet 108
club R 16
coast 77
coat pocket 108
coffee table R 107
come along 53
comedy R 25
Come on. 116
come over 45
Come to think of it
  ... R 51
come up R 2
common
  sense R 16
completely 29
confident R 49
confuse R 95
confused (past
  part) R 71
confusing (pres
  part) R 71
connect R 33
connection R 91
consult R 106
contact lenses 116
control (n) R 50
convention R 122
conversationalist R 16
cookies 76
copy (n) 44
copy (v) 45
correctly 28
cost a
  fortune R 18
cost an arm and a
  leg R 87
cough 102
cough
  medicine R 107

Could you tell me
  ... ? 84
counseling
  (n) R 15
count on
  (someone) R 42
crafts 80
crew R 24
cross (v) 84
crowd 100
custom R 26

daily R 50
dead R 96
deaf 118
death R 81
decide R 19
decision R 119
deep sleep R 24
definitely R 71
depend on 93
depressed by
  (something) 77
depressing (pres
  part) 77
depression R 50
descendant R 26
desert R 25
design (adj) R 17
diabetes R 50
dial (v) 46
Did you have
  anything special
  in mind? 36
dining (n) R 34
dinner time 68
direct (adj) 90
directing (v) R 25
director R 25
disappointed (past
  part) 76
disappointed in
  (something) 77
disappointing (pres
  part) 76
discount (adj) R 53
discover R 81
discovery R 81
disturb R 95

Supplementary vocabulary

Some irregular verbs

Simple form	Simple past	Past participle
be	was, were	been
become	became	become
begin	began	begun
break	broke	broken
bring	brought	brought
build	built	built
buy	bought	bought
catch	caught	caught
choose	chose	chosen
come	came	come
cost	cost	cost
cut	cut	cut
do	did	done
draw	drew	drawn
drink	drank	drunk
drive	drove	driven
eat	ate	eaten
fall	fell	fallen
feel	felt	felt
fight	fought	fought
find	found	found
fit	fit	fit
fly	flew	flown
forget	forgot	forgotten
get	got	gotten
give	gave	given
go	went	gone
grow	grew	grown
have	had	had
hear	heard	heard
hide	hid	hidden
hit	hit	hit
hold	held	held
hurt	hurt	hurt
keep	kept	kept
know	knew	known
leave	left	left
let	let	let

Simple form	Simple past	Past participle
lose	lost	lost
make	made	made
mean	meant	meant
meet	met	met
pay	paid	paid
put	put	put
quit	quit	quit
read	read [red]	read [red]
ride	rode	ridden
ring	rang	rung
run	ran	run
say	said	said
see	saw	seen
sell	sold	sold
send	sent	sent
set	set	set
shoot	shot	shot
shut	shut	shut
sing	sang	sung
sink	sank	sunk
sit	sat	sat
sleep	slept	slept
speak	spoke	spoken
spend	spent	spent
stand	stood	stood
steal	stole	stolen
swim	swam	swum
take	took	taken
teach	taught	taught
tear	tore	torn
tell	told	told
think	thought	thought
throw	threw	thrown
understand	understood	understood
wake	woke	woken
wear	wore	worn
win	won	won
write	wrote	written

Answers to selected exercises

Exercise 11, p. 30, from top to bottom:
United Nations, Organization of American States, North Atlantic Treaty Organization, Union of Soviet Socialist Republics

Exercise 1, p. 82:

apartment	building	large	near	street
available	evenings	location	north	suburban
bedroom	immediately	modern	room	transportation

Exercise 9, p. 101, from left to right:
Humphrey Bogart, Greta Garbo, Louis Armstrong, Amelia Earhart

134

Some parts of a house

living room	bedroom	bathroom	attic	garage	porch	closet
dining room	kitchen	basement	roof	yard	balcony	

How to read large numbers

Money	Street addresses	Telephone numbers
$1,003: a/one thousand (and) three dollars	1003 Moore Street: ten-oh-three Moore Street	858-1003: eight-five-eight–one-oh-oh-three
$1,035: a/one thousand (and) thirty-five dollars	1035 Moore Street: ten–thirty-five Moore Street	858-1035: eight-five-eight–one-oh-three-five
$1,500: fifteen hundred dollars or a/one thousand five hundred dollars	1500 Moore Street: fifteen hundred Moore Street	858-1500: eight-five-eight–one-five-hundred or eight-five-eight–one-five-oh-oh
$1,853: a/one thousand eight hundred (and) fifty-three dollars	1853 Moore Street: eighteen–fifty-three Moore Street	858-1853: eight-five-eight–one-eight-five-three
$3,200: thirty-two hundred dollars or three thousand two hundred dollars	3200 Moore Street: thirty-two hundred Moore Street	858-3200: eight-five-eight–three-two-hundred or eight-five-eight–three-two-oh-oh
$4,253: four thousand two hundred (and) fifty-three dollars	4253 Moore Street: forty-two–fifty-three Moore Street	858-4253: eight-five-eight–four-two-five-three
$10,902: ten thousand nine hundred (and) two dollars	10902 Moore Street: ten–nine-oh-two Moore Street	—
$21,500: twenty-one thousand five hundred dollars	21500 Moore Street: twenty-one–five hundred Moore Street	—
Calendar years are read the same way as street addresses.		

Some weights and measures

Weight (U.S.)	Volume (liquid measure—U.S.)	Length (U.S.)
16 ounces = 1 pound 1 ton = 2,000 pounds (U.S.) = 2,240 pounds (Great Britain)	16 fluid ounces = 1 pint 2 pints = 1 quart 4 quarts = 1 gallon	12 inches = 1 foot 3 feet = 1 yard 1,760 yards (5,280 feet) = 1 mile

Weight Equivalents		Volume (liquid measure) Equivalents	
1 ounce = 28.3 grams	1 gram = 0.035 ounce	1 ounce = 29.58 milliliters	1 milliliter = 0.035 ounce
1 pound = 0.45 kilogram	1 kilogram = 2.204 pounds	1 pint = 0.47 liter	1 liter = 2.1 pints
1 ton (U.S.) = 0.907 metric ton	1 metric ton = 1.1 tons (U.S.)	1 quart = 0.95 liter	1 liter = 1.06 quarts
		1 gallon = 3.79 liters	1 liter = 0.26 gallon

Linear Equivalents			
1 inch = 2.54 centimeters	1 yard = 0.914 meter	1 millimeter = 0.04 inch	1 meter = 3.2 feet (1.09 yards)
1 foot = 0.30 meter	1 mile = 1.6 kilometers	1 centimeter = 0.39 inch	1 kilometer = 0.62 mile

To convert from Celsius to Fahrenheit:	To convert from Fahrenheit to Celsius:
1. Multiply Celsius by 9. 2. Divide by 5. 3. Add 32.	1. Subtract 32 from Fahrenheit. 2. Multiply by 5. 3. Divide by 9.

To convert kilometers to miles per hour:	To convert miles per hour to kilometers:
1. Divide by 8. 2. Multiply by 5.	1. Divide by 5. 2. Multiply by 8.

Pronunciation

Stress and intonation

Affirmative statement: I just saw a nice apartment.

Information question: Where is it?

Yes-no question: Is it far?

Included question: Do you know where it is?

Conditional sentence: If it's nice, I'll go camping this weekend.

Affirmative statement with alternatives: You can either drive or take a bus.

Tag questions: You're hungry, aren't you?

That chicken looks good, doesn't it?

Phonetic symbols

Consonants

[p] pen, apple
[t] ten, can't
[k] coffee, like
[b] bank, cabbage
[d] dinner, idea
[g] good, again
[f] far, after
[v] very, have
[θ] think, with
[ð] the, mother
[s] some, dress
[z] zero, busy
[š] shoe, information
[ž] pleasure, measure
[č] children, teach
[j] job, age
[l] letter, mile
[r] right, hurry
[m] many, name
[n] never, money
[ŋ] ring, sing
[w] water, away
[y] year, million

Vowels

[iy] meet, tea
[i] in, visit
[ey] wait, great
[e] tell, help
[æ] ask, family
[ə] across, but
[a] father, hot
[uw] you, room
[u] could, put
[ow] home, go
[ɔ] water, long
[ay] dime, night
[aw] found, house
[ɔy] boy, join

136